MW01705651

Student Review

Introduction to Management

Student Review

Introduction to Management

THIRD EDITION

Raymond F. Attner

Jim Lee Morgan

PWS-KENT
Publishing Company • Boston

PWS-KENT
Publishing Company

PWS-KENT Publishing Company is a division of Wadsworth, Inc.

Printed in the United States of America
1 2 3 4 5 6 7 8 9—92 91 90 89

Preface

Shakespeare said, "to thine own self be true." No better guidance can be given to a student than those words. This study guide was designed with the idea that your consistent use of it would help you to not only master the course but also to begin to develop managerial talents. Of course, every educational text begins with that premise. Yet, students fail. Why? The principal reason is that students rush through books without realizing how and why they are designed as they are.

This book has a very simple idea behind it. It is a condensation of your textbook. Each chapter of the text has a corresponding chapter in the student review. You will find several features in the student review that should enhance your understanding of the textbook. First of all, the beginning of each chapter outlines certain Learning Objectives. These are statements of what the authors expect you to know once you have completed reading and discussing the text and study guide. They are brief outlines of what you will be tested on in the course.

The Overview is a condensation of the text's chapter. The purpose of the overview is not to substitute for the text materials but to give you a brief introduction to what you will study in more depth in the text. Consider the overview to be an appetizer. Each of the chapters has key vocabulary words, or Essential Terms. The study guide provides you with textbook definitions in a matching exercise that will help you learn the managerial terms you will need in your future business career.

A series of short, thought-provoking questions are contained in the Brain Teasers section. Take time to jot down your thoughts for each of the questions. You will find that they address issues raised in the Learning Objectives. Another way to check up on your understanding of the textbook materials is to answer the Rapid Review questions. They consist of fill-in-the-blank statements and true/false questions. Again, each question is structured to reinforce your understanding of the learning objectives. The last feature of each chapter is the Student Exercise. Each chapter has a suggested activity for you to undertake. Many of them will require you to visit businesses or spend time outside of class other than reading. Don't avoid the exercises. It has been our experience that students who conscientiously work through each exercise gain an insight into the world of management which cannot be duplicated in a book or classroom.

The best way to use this student review is to review the Learning Objectives and read the Overview first. Then get into the textbook. After you have read the text material, return to the student review and work through the Essential Terms and Rapid Review. Once you feel that you have mastered the basics, then enjoy the experiences you will encounter in the Student Exercise.

RAY ATTNER

JIM LEE MORGAN

Contents

CHAPTER 1	**Management: An Occupation and a Team**	**1**
CHAPTER 2	**Managing Yourself**	**9**
CHAPTER 3	**Communicating**	**17**
CHAPTER 4	**Planning: The First Function**	**24**
CHAPTER 5	**Planning Techniques**	**34**
CHAPTER 6	**Making Decisions**	**43**
CHAPTER 7	**Organizing: The Formal Organization**	**52**
CHAPTER 8	**Organizing: The Informal Organization**	**65**
CHAPTER 9	**Staffing**	**75**
CHAPTER 10	**Human Motivation**	**89**
CHAPTER 11	**Leadership**	**102**
CHAPTER 12	**Controlling: Prevention and Coping**	**113**
CHAPTER 13	**Controls**	**121**
CHAPTER 14	**Managing the Organizational Climate: Managing Change and Conflict**	**129**

CHAPTER 15 **Management and Productivity** **139**

CHAPTER 16 **Management and Society** **146**

CHAPTER 17 **International Management** **154**

CHAPTER

1 Management: An Occupation and a Team

LEARNING OBJECTIVES

After reading and discussing this chapter, you should be able to:

1. Define this chapter's essential terms.
2. Explain why managers are necessary in organizations.
3. List and briefly define the five management functions.
4. Explain the universality of management as it relates to organizations and levels of management.
5. Discuss the roles managers perform.
6. Discuss the skills required of a manager.
7. Discuss the five schools of management thought and relate each to modern-day management.

OVERVIEW

WHAT IS MANAGEMENT?

Management is one of the oldest business activities. Yet it is one of the newest disciplines of study in the business world. It has been defined as "getting things done through people." Under this definition, someone can be called a manager only if others are involved. The relationship between managers and others is central to the notion of an organization. An organization is a group of two or more persons that exists and operates to achieve clearly stated, commonly held goals. By coupling the definitions of management and of organization, two major conclusions can be drawn: management can only occur in an organization and managers are universally responsible for seeing that organizational goals are met. In short, the manager is the catalyst for all organizational activities.

MANAGEMENT LEVELS

Most organizations in today's world are large and complex. These two characteristics require managers to specialize in different functions and possess different levels of responsibilities. The highest level of management, known as top- or executive-level managers, spends most of its time addressing policy issues and developing long-range plans. Examples of top-level managers are presidents and vice presidents. The lowest level of managers is called first-line managers or supervisors. This is the level of management that directly supervises the day-to-day work of non-management personnel. In very large organizations, a middle level of management is found between top and first-line management. The major responsibility of these middle managers is to assist other managers in carrying out their decision-making responsibilities. The variety of decisions and the amount of time spent in different kinds of activities is a distinguishing characteristic of the different levels of management. It is important to remember that, at all levels of management, in all organizations, managers perform all five functions of management in varying degrees.

MANAGEMENT FUNCTIONS

The principle task of a manager is to make decisions. This leads to and is precipitated by the manager performing the five managerial functions: *planning, organizing, staffing, directing,* and *controlling.* Planning is looking at the future and determining where the organization should be in that time frame and determining how to get there. Organizing is determining what work is necessary to achieve the plan, dividing the work into jobs, and then arranging the jobs in a structure so that they are supportive of each other. Staffing is the effort to attract good people to an organization and then to develop and retain them. Directing is motivating and leading workers so that they can achieve the plan. Lastly, controlling is the checking and correcting of a plan as it is being carried out.

MANAGEMENT ROLES

Managers must be all things to all people. In the process of carrying out the functions of management, different situations arise that can require different roles. A manager is at times a figurehead, at other times a leader, and still at other times a liaison, a monitor, a disseminator of information, a spokesperson, an entrepreneur, a disturbance handler, a resource allocator, a negotiator.

MANAGEMENT SKILLS

All managers are hired for three reasons. First, they possess some technical skill. Whether it is as an electronics engineer or as an educator, the manager must have a skill of substance. Secondly, the manager must possess conceptual skills in the field of management. That is to say, you must know what management is all about and how to apply the principles of management. Last of all, every manager must have human-relations, or people, skills.

EVALUATION OF MANAGEMENT PERFORMANCE

Because managers have such diverse demands placed on them, their performance is an important concern. Two criteria are most frequently used to judge managerial performance: effectiveness and efficiency. Effectiveness is a measurement of whether an intended outcome is satisfactorily achieved. Measuring the cost of achieving a result is the domain of efficiency. A good manager will also be concerned with history as a standard for performance. Developing a good philosophical understanding of how and why things happen in an organization will serve the manager well.

MANAGEMENT THEORIES

The history of management thinking is divided into five schools of thought: the classical, behavioralist, quantitative, systems, and contingency schools.

The oldest school is the classical school, which has two parts, the "scientific management" and the "administrative" schools. Scientific management stresses improved production through work efficiency. Administrative theory emphasizes the need to find and apply universal principles of management that will be applicable to all organizations. The behaviorists also focus on increased productivity, but they believe that such improvements will come from better understanding of human behavior rather than of design of jobs. Mathematical models and the use of computers for predicting unforeseen events is at the heart of the quantitative school, which is also known as management science. Management science strives to improve decision-making by giving certainty to managers. Systems management stresses the holistic nature of organizations: problems and opportunities must be viewed from an overall organizational viewpoint. The contingency school believes that the actions or approaches managers should take depend on the situation and its variables. It looks for the most effective way to deal with any situation or problem.

MANAGEMENT: AN ART OR SCIENCE?

Management has many components which would qualify it as a science. However, it is not consistent enough to be considered a science. Yet the field is not exclusively an art—managers do not just follow their whims. Management is neither an art nor a science. The prudent manager is the one who knows when his or her practices are in the realm of certainty (science), or creativity (art).

ESSENTIAL TERMS

Match the following essential terms with the proper definition. The correct answers are located in the key at the end of the chapter.

A. conceptual skill
B. human skill
C. management
D. manager
E. organization
F. role
G. system
H. technical skill

____ 1. The ability to use the processes, the practices, the techniques, and the tools of a manager's specialty.

____ 2. The ability to view the organization as a whole and see the parts of the organization relate and depend on one another.

____ 3. A group of interrelated parts, operating as a whole, to achieve stated goals or to function according to a plan or design.

____ 4. A person who makes decisions from a position of formal authority, who will commit resources toward the achievement of a goal.

____ 5. A group of two or more people that exists and operates to achieve clearly stated, common goals.

____ 6. The ability to interact with other people successfully. To understand, work with, and relate to individuals and groups of people.

____ 7. Behaviors a manager is required to enact as he or she functions in the organizational environment. The role is influenced by the job description and the expectations of superiors, subordinates, and peers.

____ 8. The process of setting and achieving goals through the execution of five basic management activities which utilize human, financial, and material resources.

BRAIN TEASERS

Write the answers to the following "brain teasers."

1. The words organization, management, and manager have overlapping but different meanings. In what ways are the three words alike and how do they differ?

2. Briefly define the functions of management and give an example of the use of each or describe a situation where a manager would have to use each function.

3. Organizations have different levels of management. This is found everywhere. Each level of management uses the same skills but in different combinations. Can you briefly describe these phenomena and how they interrelate in terms of the concept of "universality?"

4. What is meant by "managerial roles?" Why do managers have to play roles? Select the two roles you would least like to play and the two you would most like to play. Why did you select the ones you did? Can you describe a situation where you would have to play a liked and a disliked role?

5. From the view of a manager practicing today, what positive contributions can be taken from each of the major schools of management thinking and put into use?

RAPID REVIEW

Complete the following by marking each statement either true or false. The correct answers are in the key at the end of the chapter.

________ 1. Management as a profession cannot exist outside of organizations.

________ 2. Large, complex organizations have the largest number of managers working at the "top."

________ 3. The title, "father of principles of management," is most appropriately given to Frederick W. Taylor.

________ 4. The Hawthorne Studies confirmed the significance of the management science emphasis on human behavior.

________ 5. Management is more a science than an art.

STUDENT EXERCISE

This exercise is planned to allow you to contact several managers and determine what they think about the field of management. Keep the results of this assignment because they will provide you with a good base to compare the changes in your perceptions over the semester.

STEP 1. Interview at least three managers. One should be employed at a large store (such as a department store), another at a small business (such as McDonald's), and one should be from local government (see your city hall).

STEP 2. Develop a series of questions to ask each manager. Things you may wish to pursue include: How do you know what future demands will be placed on your organization? Have you made any internal organizational changes because of these expectations? Have these affected your hiring or training practices? Have you experienced any problems in motivating your employees? If so, what were they and why did they occur? How do you go about planning your activities? How do you know when you are on target in meeting your plans? Note: Don't use managerial words, see if they do!

When you are finished, look at the three sets of responses. Which of the managers is the best one, in your opinion? Why? What would you do differently if you were in their places?

ANSWER KEY

ESSENTIAL TERMS

1. H	3. G	5. E	7. F
2. A	4. D	6. B	8. C

RAPID REVIEW

1. True
2. False
3. False
4. False
5. False

CHAPTER

2 Managing Yourself

LEARNING OBJECTIVES

After reading and discussing this chapter, you should be able to:

1. Define this chapter's essential terms.
2. Describe the importance of, and the means for getting to know your skills, aptitudes, interests, and motivations.
3. Discuss the concept of obsolescence as it relates to your career and what you can do to prevent it.
4. Outline the steps you can take in planning for your future growth and development.
5. Describe the five basic steps you can use to plan your career.
6. Describe the four basic stages you can expect your career to pass through.
7. Describe the socialization process you can expect to experience with each new employer.

OVERVIEW

GETTING TO KNOW YOURSELF

In order to be a successful manager, you must look at what it takes to be a good manager and at who you are. The best way to determine whether or not you may be capable of being a manager is to take an inventory of your skills, aptitudes, interests, and motivations.

DETERMINING YOUR SKILLS AND APTITUDES. Skills are mental or muscular-motor abilities. They are usually measured through proficiency tests and exercises. Aptitudes are natural tendencies or talents. These are areas of a person's personality which may or may not be developed. Both skills and aptitudes can be extended and developed by hard work and study.

DETERMINING YOUR INTERESTS. An interest is an area of work or activity that has a special personal appeal. It is something that captures your attention, curiosity, or fancy.

DETERMINING YOUR MOTIVATIONS. A motivation is a psychological need. It may be a need for recognition, status, security, or many other concerns. Prospective managers must decide what is important to them and whether a given job can meet their needs.

Looking at one's skills, aptitudes, interests, and motivations is an important first step before entering management, as well as a step that should be continually revised. Keeping an inventory of these items is important to see if you can be satisfied in a given work environment as well as to see how you change over the years.

EDUCATION AND OBSOLESCENCE

One of the major reasons people fail to advance in their careers is obsolescence. A long-range plan to avoid becoming obsolete includes recognizing the value of education and obtaining it.

AVOIDING OBSOLESCENCE. Obsolescence is when something is outdated. People, like machines, can become obsolete. The first step in avoiding obsolescence is to continue to check out your inventory of skills, aptitudes, interests, and motivations. If you see a deficit, then you may need additional training, education, or experience. Additionally, technical knowledge must be continually updated. This is also true of managerial and human relations abilities and skills.

EDUCATION AND INCOME. Not only can obsolescence be avoided by acquiring education, but in the long run education pays for itself. Workers with college degrees have more than twice the monthly income of those with only a high school diploma. Although the actual dollars earned each year may change, the size of the gap between the groups tends to stay about the same over the years.

PLANS FOR IMPROVEMENT

The manager's first function is to plan. This is also true in your professional life. You must recognize that the skills you take away from this course or your college career will become obsolete in a very short time. Thus, like the careful motorist who looks after the maintenance of her automobile, you must watch after your career and the things that will make it successful. A good outline to follow in plotting your career follows below.

CONSTRUCTING YOUR PLAN. Your plan should answer the questions who, what, how, when, where, and how much. This means that you must realistically evaluate where you are now and determine what you must do to get to where you want to be. Be honest when constructing your plan.

SETTING A TIMETABLE. A plan has no meaning unless it has deadlines. You must set and follow realistic schedules that will govern what you want to achieve.

IMPLEMENTING YOUR PLANS. Once a solid plan has been established and a realistic schedule set, the next step is to see that it is carried out. If you stumble, don't get upset. Recognize why you were not able to reach your plan, try to improve your efforts, and continue on the path you have outlined if it is a reasonable course of action.

OVERCOMING THE BARRIERS TO IMPROVEMENT. A wise man once said that we have met the enemy and he is us. The greatest barrier to your achieving your plan will be yourself. This is because it is human nature to tire of a routine. Develop habits that will enable you to continue despite setbacks. This can be made easier if you work at creating strong support groups. This means that you must work at cultivating good friends and keeping family relations in repair. Also, you should recognize that your employer will be different from you and make demands of you. View your employer as you would a teacher. In most cases, your boss will not only be a good model to follow but will also be an extension of your "support group." This is because your boss has a vested interest in your success.

PLANNING YOUR CAREER

In order to practice effective career planning, it is necessary for you to set goals. As part of this career planning, it is necessary to think seriously about all of the elements of a career, research why people quit jobs they actively sought, and discover what it takes to be successful in a management job.

THINKING ABOUT CAREERS. Experts in career planning offer some general advice for long-range success. The points to consider include: thinking about the position you want to hold when you retire and then working back from there, talking to a person who holds that final job and finding out what career path he or she followed, and avoiding looking for a next job until you have decided where you want to be in the long run. In addition, it is wise to try to identify potential trouble areas in every situation, take on an undesirable assignment, keep your word, continuously propose ideas, find people you can learn from, and associate with positive people.

WHY PEOPLE QUIT JOBS. The number one reason people quit jobs is having a poor opportunity for advancement. Other reasons for quitting jobs include: wrong fit of the person and the job, displeasure with the kind of supervision received, dissatisfaction with pay, and personal problems.

MAKING IT IN MANAGEMENT. Surveys of personnel directors, top-level executives, and middle managers have identified a number of factors perceived as necessary for making it in management. The factors identified include: experience and knowledge in the field, technical skills and appropriate level of educational achievement, ability to manage, communication skills, willingness to work hard, good job performance, luck, an entrepreneurial spirit, ability to manage intracompany rivalry, a thorough knowledge of one's company and its markets, the ability to identify a successful strategy and to stick with it, adeptness at identifying and solving problems before they become obstacles, and flexibility.

THE SEQUENCE OF PLANNING STEPS. The foregoing has talked about how to put yourself in the best position to be a good manager. The following is a sequence of five steps to plan your career.

1. Identify your career objectives.
2. Then analyze different jobs and how they fit into career paths.
3. Next, after knowing what kinds of jobs you are willing to accept, identify possible employers.
4. Then, get to work and apply for and obtain employment.
5. Lastly, continue to assess your progress, in terms of your career plans, and reassess your present situation.

YOUR PRESENT JOB. Chances are good that your motivations and career objectives may have changed since the start of your present job. Before you decide whether your choice of employment has been satisfactory, give yourself at least one full year in the job. Don't leave your present position before you know where you want to go and have secured that position.

CAREER STAGES

A career is not one continuous sequence. There may be many changes and most often different, distinct phases will be passed through. Four of the most common career phases are:

TRIAL STAGE. This is the first stage, when a person becomes serious about seeking employment and "tries out" different jobs. This may be a "trial-and-error" phase or it can be a successful first job.

ESTABLISHMENT AND ADVANCEMENT. Once a job is found that offers both a challenge and an opportunity for growth, most persons will make a commitment to stay in that field and take actions that will enable them to grow. Growth leads to advancement and the beginning of a career.

MIDCAREER. Once we have made a career commitment, there is a ladder that must be climbed. One of the frustrations is finding oneself moving too slowly or finding work being different than we had planned for. This is often known as the "mid-career crisis" and can be the beginning of a new career or an adjustment in plans.

LATE CAREER. Towards the end of one's work career, post-work activities become important. Retirement is more than not having to work. It is a time which must also be planned just as one's work career has been. Additionally, the professional manager will also be concerned about grooming his or her replacements prior to retirement so that the organization can continue to function well.

ADJUSTING TO YOUR EMPLOYER

We all enter work with high expectations. However, the work world, like the rest of life, is less than perfect. You will undoubtedly encounter employers who will grate on your nerves and cause problems for you. It is important to recognize the dynamics of what causes these types of disruptions in the work world.

THE SOCIALIZATION PROCESS. When you join a new organization, you must recognize that the organization has a set of values and norms for behavior that reflect the personality of the company. Edgar Schein has described this process for a new employee as being the creation of expectations, adjusting to what an organization really believes in, and mutually accepting each other. If you cannot go through the socialization process, it may be best to leave a given organization.

INSIDERS' DEMANDS. In all organizations, you are subject to superiors, subordinates, and peers. Each group makes demands on you. Since they are part of the organization, these "insiders" must be dealt with. Like it or not, their demands count for something. Such things as loyalty, time, support, and team play will be expected of you.

OUTSIDERS' DEMANDS. Perhaps the most difficult demand to deal with is that which the young manager often encounters: demands from those you love, members of your support group, and work interests. It is foolhardy not to recognize that outsider demands must be met not only to maintain support group relations but to make sure that you have adequate leisure, rest, relaxation, and diversity in your life.

ACHIEVING A BALANCE. Everything said up to this point suggests that the world you are about to enter is a demanding one. Finding the right combination of work and work-related growth activities, your personal life, and your spiritual and mental needs must be identified and always kept in balance. Sacrificing one element of your life for another usually is not a good policy.

TAKING CHARGE OF YOUR FUTURE

Improvement, both personally and professionally, comes through learning. Learning is transmitted through planned experiences or random happenings. You can only learn from the latter if you develop skills which enable you to listen and observe and to be aware of events and how others handled those events. Planned experiences give you a better opportunity for taking control of your life. By developing an educational and professional growth plan, you have greater chances of success. However, you can do that only if you know yourself.

Learn! Take charge of your future!

ESSENTIAL TERMS

Match the following essential terms with the proper definition. The correct answer is located in the key at the end of the chapter.

A. aptitude
B. interest
C. obsolescence
D. skill
E. socialization

____ 1. The condition in which a person or a machine is no longer capable of performing to management's expectations.

____ 2. Mental or muscular-motor ability to do something well.

____ 3. The process through which new members of an organization gain exposure to its values and norms, its policies and procedures, and the behavior expected from new people.

____ 4. A fundamental capacity or talent that may be innate or acquired.

____ 5. Areas of activity that capture your imagination and curiosity and have a special appeal.

BRAIN TEASERS

Write the answers to the following "brain teasers."

1. Of the skills, interests, aptitudes, and motivations you now possess, which do you believe will most aid you in developing managerial abilities? Why? Which could use some improvement? Why?

2. Describe how you see your career moving through the four phases most careers move through. To what must you be most attuned to make each career phase rewarding and fulfilling to you?

3. What can become obsolete with you or another person? How can you guard against obsolescence?

4. What do you consider to be the relationship between ethics and the socialization process? Is there a potential conflict? How so?

5. How would you go about counseling a friend to develop a plan for career development?

RAPID REVIEW

Complete the following sentences with the appropriate words. The correct answers are in the key at the end of the chapter.

1. A ________ ________ is a listing of the positive and negative characteristics you possess and is the first step in getting to know yourself.
2. Matching a job's rewards and a person's needs can best be done by finding out what a person's ________ are.
3. Friends, family, and others close to you comprise what is known as a ________ ________, which is a critical element in planning your career.
4. Your ________ may be the most valuable asset in your career or a major barrier to work around.
5. The ________ ________ ________ is a U.S. Department of Labor publication that can help you determine which jobs match your personal qualifications.

STUDENT EXERCISE

This exercise is designed to help you understand where you are now in your life and where you want to be in the future.

STEP 1. Take a piece of paper and draw a straight line from one side to the other. That line represents your life and is finite. Your beginning is on the left side and your ending on the right side. Pick a spot on the line where you think you are today. Make a mark there.

STEP 2. List experiences you have had in the past that you consider to be successes. Do the same for your failures. Are there common patterns or elements that consistently appear?

STEP 3. List the things you would like to accomplish in the future. What skills or abilities will assist you in achieving those goals?

STEP 4. Compare the qualities you now possess—those which have led to successes and disappointments—to the strengths you will need in the future.

STEP 5. Ask yourself the following questions: What factors encouraged you to develop a skill in the past? When certain inabilities led to failure, what steps have you taken to overcome those deficiencies? What must you do to develop needed skills in the future? How do you feel about yourself after reading this chapter and doing this exercise? Do you feel more confident about your future?

ANSWER KEY

ESSENTIAL TERMS

1. C
2. D
3. E
4. A
5. B

RAPID REVIEW

1. personal inventory
2. interests
3. support group
4. employer
5. Occupational Outlook Quarterly

CHAPTER

3 Communicating

LEARNING OBJECTIVES

After reading and discussing this chapter, you should be able to:

1. Define this chapter's terms.
2. Diagram the communication process, and explain the importance and relationship of each component to the others.
3. Explain the responsibilities of the sender and receiver in the communication process.
4. List and explain the barriers to communication, and suggest remedies to overcome these barriers.
5. List and briefly explain the Ten Commandments of Good Communication.

OVERVIEW

WHAT IS COMMUNICATION?

Communication is the transmission of information and understanding from one person or group to another. The goal of communication is to convey as much "like" information as possible. If common understanding exists after communication has occurred, then it can be said that an effective job of communication has taken place.

THE COMMUNICATION PROCESS

Communication involves two or more people in a very delicate process. The process itself is filled with problems. The sender, the person who wishes to send a signal to another, has a message, or information, to transmit. The sender must select a medium, a means by which the message will be forwarded to the receiver, the person or persons to whom the message is addressed. Once the message arrives, the receiver must decode the message and interpret it. The receiver uses feedback either to prompt clarification or to let the sender know the message has been received as intended.

COMMUNICATION RESPONSIBILITIES

The sender and receiver have responsibilities in the communication process.

SENDER RESPONSIBILITIES. The five responsibilities of the sender are:

1. Be sure of the purpose of communication.
2. Know the receiver.
3. Construct the message with the receiver in mind.
4. Select the proper medium.
5. Time the messages correctly.

Medium selection requires that the sender recognize how the receiver will perceive the message as well as understanding the importance of clarity in the message. When a written document is sent without your directly contacting the receiver, the communication is impersonal. Personal communications involves human contact between the sender and receiver. The problem with impersonal communication is that it does not afford the sender an opportunity to receive immediate feedback, which is the receiver's reaction to the sender's message. Obviously, personal communication allows feedback but cuts into time the sender has for other tasks.

RECEIVER RESPONSIBILITIES. The receiver also has responsibilities. They are:

1. Listen actively to the sender.
2. Be sensitive to the sender.
3. Indicate the appropriate medium for the sender to use.
4. Initiate feedback.

COMMUNICATION BARRIERS

Even with the best of efforts, there are roadblocks to good communications. These are called communication barriers. Some barriers arise in interpersonal, face-to-face communications, while others are unique to organizational structures.

INTERPERSONAL OR FACE-TO-FACE BARRIERS. There are eight common barriers to face-to-face communication:

1. Hearing what we expect to hear.
2. Ignoring information that conflicts with what we know.

3. Evaluating the source.
4. Differing perceptions.
5. Words having different meanings for different people.
6. Conflicting nonverbal communication.
7. Emotional environment interfering with reason and understanding.
8. Noise.

ORGANIZATIONAL BARRIERS. Besides the interpersonal barriers to communication, other blocks arise because of the nature of organizations:

1. Management levels.
2. Number of people supervised.
3. Rank or position in the organization.
4. Change in managers.
5. Managers' interpretations.

TEN COMMANDMENTS OF GOOD COMMUNICATION

As you begin to develop an awareness of your written and spoken patterns, use these guidelines for further improvements:

1. Seek to clarify your ideas before communicating.
2. Examine the true purpose of your communication.
3. Consider the total physical and human setting whenever you communicate.
4. Consult with others, when appropriate, in planning communications.
5. Be aware of the overtones of your message when you communicate.
6. Take the opportunity, when it arises, to convey something of help or value to the receiver.
7. Follow up your communication; don't just dictate.
8. Communicate for tomorrow as well as today.
9. Be sure that your actions support your communications.
10. Seek not only to be understood but to understand—be a good listener.

Communication is the most important tool that a manager has. To use it successfully requires a commitment to and an understanding of those in the work force. To use it unsuccessfully requires nothing other than writing, speaking, reading, or listening without regard for others.

ESSENTIAL TERMS

Match the following essential terms with the proper definition. The correct answers are located in the key at the end of the chapter.

A. communication
B. communication barrier
C. feedback
D. impersonal communication
E. interpersonal communication
F. medium
G. message
H. receiver
I. sender

____ 1. A receiver's reaction to a message through which a receiver becomes a sender.

____ 2. The transmission of information and understanding from one person or group to another.

____ 3. The person(s) initiating a message.

____ 4. The method chosen to deliver a message.

____ 5. The information being transmitted in the communication process.

____ 6. The person(s) intended as the audience for a message.

____ 7. Communication delivered either face-to-face or by voice-to-voice.

____ 8. Objects or behaviors that can interfere with communication effectiveness.

____ 9. Communication in which the participants do not interact directly.

BRAIN TEASERS

Write the answers to the following "brain teasers."

1. Diagram the communication process and list difficulties or problems associated with each component.

2. What factors, external to the communication process itself, can aid communication?

3. Which communication responsibilities of the sender and receiver overlap? Why? Are there any responsibilities that are unique only to the sender or receiver? Why?

4. Describe the six barriers you consider most significant in blocking communication and explain why you feel they are the most important. How would you avoid or overcome them?

5. What is the purpose of having a list, such as the Ten Commandments of Good Communication? Why don't individuals follow such a list when communicating?

RAPID REVIEW

Complete the following sentences with the appropriate word. The correct answers are located in the key at the end of the chapter.

1. The selection of words or symbols is done to benefit the ________________'s needs.
2. Communication problems can be partially avoided by appealing to the best of the receiver's vocabularies, which consist of the ________________, ________________, ________________, and ________________ vocabulary.
3. Memos, letters, directives and other kinds of written messages are examples of ________________ communication.
4. Asking for clarification of a message is an example of ________________.
5. Different experiences, values, and beliefs can cause differing ________________ of the world.

STUDENT EXERCISE

This exercise is planned to acquaint you with some of the barriers that block communication, as well as to introduce the "creative listening" process.

STEP 1. Read an article on a controversial subject. Ask a friend to read the same article.

STEP 2. Prepare a written critique of the article and ask your friend to do the same without conferring.

STEP 3. Read each other's critiques and discuss the various points that were made.
A. Before you can make a statement regarding something the other has said, each must summarize what the other has said. Then state your position. You may ask clarifying questions but you cannot make a statement until you have summarized, to your friend's satisfaction, what your friend said.
B. Continue this process for at least twenty minutes.

STEP 4. Did you gain a better understanding of each other's position and why you each believe what you do? What communication barriers did you notice in your exchange?

ANSWER KEY

ESSENTIAL TERMS

1. C	3. I	5. G	7. E	9. D
2. A	4. F	6. H	8. B	

RAPID REVIEW

1. receiver
2. written, spoken, heard, visual
3. impersonal
4. feedback
5. perceptions

CHAPTER

4 Planning: The First Function

LEARNING OBJECTIVES

After reading and discussing this chapter, you should be able to:

1. Define this chapter's essential terms.
2. Explain the importance of planning and its relationship to the other management functions.
3. Differentiate the planning responsibilities of the three levels of management.
4. Explain the difference between strategic and operating planning.
5. List and discuss the seven basic steps in the planning process.
6. Discuss the major barriers to effective planning.
7. Discuss the aids to successful planning.

OVERVIEW

WHY DO YOU NEED A PLAN?

Most managers and organizations cannot afford the luxury of trial and error; it is too costly in terms of the resources expended. Planning helps avoid errors, waste, and delays; and it aids our efforts to become both effective and efficient.

PLANNING DEFINED

Planning is preparing for tomorrow today. It is the activity that allows managers to determine what they want and how to get it. Planning answers six basic questions in regard to any intended activity: what (the goal or goals), when (the time frame in which it will be accomplished), where (the place or places where the plans or planning will reach its conclusion), who (which people will perform the tasks), how (the specific steps or methods to reach the goals), and how much (resources necessary to reach the goals).

IMPORTANCE OF PLANNING

THE PRIMARY MANAGEMENT FUNCTION. Planning is often called the first function because it must be undertaken before other functions. It sets the stage for resource acquisition and the focus of energy for the entire organization. It provides direction and a common sense of purpose.

IMPACT ON OTHER MANAGEMENT FUNCTIONS. The organization structure is developed to support the objectives created during planning. Staffing is done in response to planning. The communication and direction provided to employees result from guidelines developed during planning. Planning provides the foundation for control because it specifies what is to be accomplished and provides a standard for measuring progress.

ABILITY TO ADJUST. Planning enables managers to adjust the organization to the environment, instead of merely reacting to it. This in turn allows for less wear and tear on the organization and its members.

UNIFIED FRAMEWORK OF PLANS. Finally, planning establishes a unified framework in which the organization can function. All managers should develop plans that support the accomplishment of other managers' plans.

TYPES AND USES OF PLANS

All managers are involved in planning and the development of plans. The kinds of plans developed and the amount of time managers spend on planning depend on the level of management they occupy. The specific types of plans developed by managers include the following.

STRATEGIC PLANS. A strategic plan develops the direction for the entire organization. The strategic plan looks ahead over the next two, three, five, or more years. The development of the plan requires involvement by all the managerial levels of the organization. The result of creating a strategic plan is a unified sense of purpose for the organization.

TACTICAL PLANS. A tactical plan is concerned with what the lower-level units within each division must do, how they must do it, and who will have the responsibility for doing it. Tactical plans are the means for achieving the strategic plans. They are concerned with shorter time frames and cover a narrower scope.

OPERATING PLANS. An operating plan is one that a manager uses to accomplish his or her job responsibilities. It can be classified as either a single-use plan or an ongoing plan. Single-use plans include programs (the who, what, where, when, how and how much for a particular activity) and budgets (which predict the sources and amounts of income and how they are to be used). Once the purpose of a single-use plan is achieved its existence is terminated.

Ongoing plans retain their value over a period of years. They are likely to cover the handling of continuing situations, problems, and activities. Ongoing plans include policies (a broad guideline for managers to follow when dealing with important areas of decision-making), procedures (a set of step-by-step directions in which activities or tasks are to be carried out), and rules (do and don't statements for controlling human behavior and conduct at work).

PLANNING PROCESSES

In order for managers to develop plans they need to employ the proper sequence of steps or processes. The type of plan being developed—strategic or operating—dictates the proper planning process to follow.

BASIC PLANNING CONCEPT. Regardless of the type of plan being developed, there is a basic planning concept the manager uses for a framework. This framework provides the answers to four questions:

- What do we want to do?
- Where are we in relation to that goal?
- Which factors will help or hinder us in reaching the goal?
- What alternatives are available to us to reach the goal and which one is best?

With these questions in mind the manager can undertake either the operating planning process or the strategic planning process, depending on the plan needed.

OPERATING PLANNING PROCESS. The operating planning process includes:

- Setting objectives—establishing short- and long-range targets.
- Analyzing and evaluating the environment—analyzing the present position and resources available to achieve objectives.
- Determining alternatives—constructing a list of possible courses of action that will lead you to your goals.
- Evaluating the alternatives—listing and considering the advantages and disadvantages of each of your possible courses of action.
- Selecting the best solution—selecting the course of action that has the most advantages and fewest disadvantages.
- Implementing the plan—determining who will be involved, what resources will be assigned, how the plan will be evaluated, and the reporting procedures.
- Controlling and evaluating the results—making certain that the plan is going according to expectations and making necessary adjustments.

STRATEGIC PLANNING PROCESS. The strategic planning process is the "big-picture" approach to planning. It sets the direction for the organization. It also provides for supportive subunit goals through multi-level involvement in the planning process. Steps in the *strategic planning process* include:

- Defining the central concept of the business—top-level management determines the type of business, industry, or mission of the organization.
- Establishing objectives for the organization—top-level management determines where the organization will focus its energy—profits, growth, survival.
- Analyzing and evaluating the environment—top-level management assesses the external and internal climate the company operates in.
- Developing sub-units' goals—using top-level management's goals as a guide, middle-level management is requested to develop its own goals.
- Comparing lower-level goals and closing the gap—middle-level management's goals are reviewed to determine if they fit and are compatible with top-level management's goals.
- Deciding on a plan—the management team decides which of the various alternative plans to use.
- Implementing the plan—all the various sub-groups (middle-level managers, and first-level managers) proceed with the detail work—who, when, and where.
- Controlling and evaluating—the progress of the plan is monitored at all levels of management.

MAKING PLANS EFFECTIVE

All managers want their plans to be effective, to yield the desired results. A step toward achieving this goal is to identify the potential barriers to successful planning and work to overcome them.

RECOGNIZE THE PLANNING BARRIERS. Planning barriers include the inability to plan (limited conceptual skills or lack of training), improper planning process (limited exposure to the idea of planning), lack of commitment to the planning process (refusal to undertake planning or fear of failure), improper information (insufficient, out-of-date, or poor-quality data with which to plan), focusing on the present at the expense of the future (failure to consider the long term because of emphasis on the short term), too much reliance on the planning department (viewing the planning department as the planners rather than as the resource for planning), and concentrating on only the controllable variables (limited acknowledgment of presence of outside variables in the planning process).

USE THE AIDS TO PLANNING. Aids to planning include acquiring as much information as possible (quantity and quality of data within the limits of time and money), using multiple sources of information (broadening the number of sources of data to eliminate tunnel vision), and involving others in the planning process (employees who have the ability and interest to contribute).

ESSENTIAL TERMS

Match the following essential terms with the proper definitions. The correct answers are located in the key at the end of the chapter.

A. budget
B. mission
C. objective
D. operating plan
E. planning
F. policy
G. procedure
H. program
I. rule
J. strategic plan
K. strategic planning
L. tactical plan

____ 1. A plan designed to achieve strategic goals.

____ 2. A plan intended to provide managers with guidelines for making decisions.

____ 3. A single-use plan for solving a problem or accomplishing a group of related activities needed to reach a goal.

____ 4. A plan designed to predict resources and amounts of income and how it is to be used.

____ 5. Planning that focuses on organizational direction.

____ 6. A plan intended to dictate human behavior or conduct at work (do's and don'ts).

____ 7. A decision about long-range plans and courses of action to achieve those goals.

____ 8. The central purpose behind the organization's existence.

_____ 9. Plans intended to answer the question "how to do something."

_____ 10. Setting objectives and determining the means (courses of action) to reach those objectives.

_____ 11. A plan that focuses on the implementation or ongoing part of a manager's planning responsibilities.

_____ 12. A target for the energy and efforts of the organization.

BRAIN TEASERS

Write the answers to the following "brain teasers."

1. Discuss planning. Include in your discussion a working definition of planning and of the importance of planning.

2. Compare operating plans and strategic plans. Include in your comparison the purposes, time frames, and scope of the plans.

3. Compare single-use plans to ongoing plans. Include in your answer the purposes of each and two examples of each type of plan.

4. Explain the purpose of the following types of plans and give an example of each.
   A. Policy—Purpose:

      Example:

   B. Rule—Purpose:

Example:

C. Procedure—Purpose:

Example:

5. Discuss the strategic planning process. Include in your discussion the purposes of the process, the steps involved, and an explanation of each step.

RAPID REVIEW

Complete the following sentences with the appropriate words. The correct answers are located in the key at the end of the chapter.

1. A manager can improve the chances of a plan's succeeding by ________________, ________________, and ________________.
2. A barrier to planning in which a manager expresses a fear of failure is known as ________________.
3. Planning is preparing for ________________.
4. ________________ plans focus on the direction of the organization while ________________ plans help to implement strategic plans.
5. Planning impacts the organizing function by ________________ from which to design an organization structure.

STUDENT EXERCISE

This exercise is designed to give you an opportunity to apply the planning process and develop a plan.

You are faced with the problem of planning your family's vacation for the next year. Using the planning process, develop the what, where, when, who, how, and how much.

STEP 1. Determine your objective.

STEP 2. Analyze and evaluate the environment.

- Evaluate where you are now:
  What do you like and not like?
  Where have you been?
  How much money do you have?
  What do the others think?
- Evaluate aids and hindrances:
  What is the economy like?
  How much time do you have?
  What commitments do you have?

STEP 3. Develop a list of alternative choices, evaluate each, and decide on a vacation.

STEP 4. Implement the plan.

- Determine what separate steps have to be accomplished for the plan to work, for example—dog in kennel, travel plans, accommodations.
- Determine the time frames necessary to *make sure* your plan works.
- Determine who will perform each task and assign responsibility.
- Determine the final cost of the plan.

ANSWER KEY

ESSENTIAL TERMS

1. L	3. H	5. K	7. J	9. G	11. D
2. F	4. A	6. I	8. B	10. E	12. C

RAPID REVIEW

1. acquiring as much information as possible, using multiple sources of information, and involving others
2. lack of commitment to the planning process
3. tomorrow today
4. strategic, tactical
5. establishing the objectives

CHAPTER

5 Planning Techniques

LEARNING OBJECTIVES

After reading and discussing this chapter, you should be able to:

1. Define this chapter's essential terms.
2. List and describe the interrelationships among the three variables in planning.
3. Discuss the nature of the managerial planning environment.
4. List and describe five quantitative tools or techniques discussed in this chapter.
5. List and describe four general planning tools or techniques discussed in this chapter.

OVERVIEW

DETERMINING DEGREES OF CERTAINTY

Plans depend to some extent on three basic elements: objectives (the stated ends a manager wishes to achieve), assumptions (the premises or conditions managers accept as true and real), and forecasts (expectations the planners formulate with regard to the likely or probable state of events or conditions at some time in the future). Assumptions are used to develop forecasts.

FORECASTING. Forecasting concentrates on predicting the probable outcomes of the activities of the organization. Forecasts may be developed by utilizing either internal organizational sources (committees and managers), and/or external organizational sources (government bureaus, agencies, and universities).

A FEW EXAMPLES. Nearly every producer of goods and services needs up-to-date market research to help decide what product will sell to whom, in how many units, with what options, and at what price. There are hundreds of market research companies developing thousands of market research reports each year for clients. In addition to research firms, another approach to forecasting is the Delphi technique where a panel of outside experts is polled or interviewed at regular intervals and paid for its forecasts.

THE PLANNING ENVIRONMENT

When managers forecast, they are trying to predict the future. The dilemma in this situation is that managers cannot hold the future constant: it is ever-changing. In addition, managers must deal with the dimension of time—the longer the period of time a forecast covers, the more vulnerable it is to elements of uncertainty. Managers use planning techniques to reduce uncertainty, increase accuracy, and help organizational leaders think through a plan prior to implementation. Planning techniques or tools are classified as either quantitative techniques or general techniques.

QUANTITATIVE PLANNING TOOLS AND TECHNIQUES

Quantitative planning tools rely on numerical data. The specific quantitative tools or techniques include the following.

NETWORKS. Networks are used to show all the activities needed to complete a project and to enable the planner to calculate the length of time the project will take from start to finish. Networks help planners to focus on the most time-consuming activities in a project, be it clerical or manufacturing. Once a project begins, the time each activity takes may vary from the time scheduled for it, and adjustments to the network's times may then be made. As networks are developed the activities create paths through the diagrams. The longest path through the diagram is known as the critical path.

OPERATIONS RESEARCH / MANAGEMENT SCIENCE TECHNIQUES. Operations research/management science techniques utilize mathematics and science to develop models that are able to provide information to forecast changes, determine the outcome of alternative courses of action, and provide analyses of the alternatives. Operations research techniques include the following.

Simulation models attempt to duplicate a part of real life operations by providing a replica of the real environment, as in the use of rocket simulations for training astronauts. Applications may be found in any situation where experimentation can take place without interruption of normal operations.

A linear program attempts to determine the best way to allocate resources when given the possible alternate uses for and limitations on the resources. Applications may be found in problems requiring the determination of costs in time or money connected with a set of alternatives. Examples include determining the fastest or least costly method of shipping goods or what quantity of resources is to be allocated to one product.

Queueing or *waiting line models* are used to help managers decide what length of waiting line or queue is preferable. It balances the cost of the line (customer dissatisfaction) against the cost of opening another line. Applications may be found in supermarkets, toll gates, or truck docks.

Game theory attempts to predict how rational people will behave in competitive situations. The purpose of the prediction is to allow strategies to be devised to counter the behavior. Game theory has application in situations in which organizations compete against each other in price, product development, advertising, and distribution systems.

BREAKEVEN ANALYSIS. Breakeven analysis is used to help businesses determine at what point their sales revenue or income will allow them to pay all their bills—their breakeven point—and, therefore, at what point income from sales will exceed expenses thus yielding a profit. It has three main elements: fixed costs (costs separate from the costs of manufacturing and selling a product), variable costs (costs connected with the manufacturing or the sale of a product), and the revenue or income connected with each unit of sales.

BUDGETING. Budgeting is used to formalize in writing the financial resources to be allocated for specific purposes. It relates the income and expected expenses for a period. Budgets can be determined through grassroots budgeting (the lowest levels of an organization prepare detailed budget information, which is then consolidated and approved at a higher level) or top-down budgeting (top-level management determines the budget and allocates it). Additionally, budgets can be developed through the historical approach (the amount budgeted the previous year is established as the base figure and adjusted upward on the basis of projected percentages) or zero-base budgets (each part of an organization is required to justify specifically each of the operations it wishes to fund).

GENERAL PLANNING TOOLS AND TECHNIQUES

General planning tools and techniques involve the talents of people in various situations. They utilize the stores of experience, expertise, energy, and creativity of people at all levels in an organization to generate potential ideas and alternatives. The specific tools or techniques include the following.

CONSULTANTS. Consultants are outside experts who are called upon to examine an organization's procedures and policies; to analyze, solve, or recommend solutions to problems; and to provide the forecasts that become the manager's assumptions for planning. They bring objective viewpoints and analyses to bear on an issue or situation. They are unaffected by the infighting and politics of the organization they are hired to serve.

COMMITTEES. A committee is a group of people who volunteer or are appointed to serve as investigators, problem solvers, or decision makers. Members bring with them the expertise, experience, and other resources needed for successfully completing their tasks. Committees may be temporary (ad hoc) or permanent (standing). Temporary committees may deal with one issue, and once it is resolved, the committee dissolves. Standing committees deal with continuing problems areas such as budgeting and safety.

BRAINSTORMING. The purpose of brainstorming is to utilize a group effort for generating ideas and alternatives that can assist management in making decisions or solving problems. The participants in brainstorming sessions are usually employees of the organization. During the course of the session no idea offered is criticized. The environment is designed to encourage and allow the free flow of ideas. After the session, ideas are sorted and the best are examined in more detail by the manager who called the session, or by the original group, or another group of experts.

PROJECT MANAGEMENT. Project management is a planning technique that involves the overseeing of a project by a project manager who must plan, organize, staff, direct and control those tasks needed to reach the desired outcome. Project teams usually consist of people from several departments or divisions. They normally cross organizational lines and borrow from several functional areas. In managing the project team, the project manager must worry about three basic things: the time a project will take, the cost of the project, and the quality of performance needed to reach the outcome specified for the project.

CRISIS TEAMS. A crisis team usually consists of key people throughout an organization who can take charge of the organization and make decisions rapidly when an unforeseen, large problem occurs. Normally, the chief executive, the top legal officer, a public relations specialist, and heads of departments that are affected by the crisis come together to analyze and decide on strategy and tactics. The concept is designed to quickly gather the key decision makers and develop a response to the problem without the normal slowdown caused by organizational levels and procedures.

WORKER PARTICIPATION TECHNIQUES. Worker participation techniques are founded on the concept that those who perform jobs and execute tasks can be extremely useful in uncovering ways in which jobs and tasks can be improved and made more efficient. An example of worker participation programs is provided by the *quality circle,* which is a cooperative effort of workers and supervisor to find ways to improve operations and quality.

Quality circles in most companies have several things in common:

- They hinge on commitments by all company personnel.
- They involve workers on a voluntary basis.
- They are administered at the supervisory levels of most firms.
- Sessions are held regularly to focus on only one problem that the supervisor or participants wish to consider.
- Updates are furnished to all participants regularly.

MANAGEMENT BY OBJECTIVES. Management by objectives (MBO) is a one-on-one approach to improving performances of both individuals and the organization as a whole. Each manager and each individual jointly develop goals. The goals are created through a negotiation process. After the goals are agreed upon they are prioritized and time-framed. Follow-up sessions are conducted in order to check progress, make adjustments if needed, and acquire additional resources. Individuals are evaluated on the number of goals they achieve, how they achieve them, and how their performances have improved.

ESSENTIAL TERMS

Match the following essential terms with the proper definitions. The correct answers are located in the key at the end of the chapter.

A. assumptions
B. brainstorming
C. breakeven analysis
D. budgeting
E. committee
F. crisis team
G. critical path
H. Delphi technique
I. fixed costs
J. forecast
K. game theory
L. linear programming
M. network
N. project management
O. quality circle
P. queueing (waiting line) models
Q. simulation
R. variable costs

_____ 1. The longest path through a production flow chart or diagram from start to finish.

_____ 2. A general planning technique involving workers and their supervisors in ways to improve methods, reduce waste and costs, and improve quality.

_____ 3. The premises or conditions that planners accept as or know to be true or real.

_____ 4. A quantitative planning technique using activities and events to chart the flow of a project from start to finish and calculate the shortest possible completion time for the project.

_____ 5. Costs unconnected to and separate from the costs of manufacturing a product or selling it.

_____ 6. A group effort at generating ideas and alternatives, using inside experts who focus their attention on one issue or problem.

_____ 7. An operations research technique that attempts to predict how people or organizations will behave in competitive situations.

_____ 8. A planning technique that attempts to formalize in writing the financial resources to be allocated for a specific purpose.

_____ 9. An operations research technique used to assist managers in deciding what length of waiting line or queue would be preferable.

_____ 10. Costs connected to the manufacture or sale of a product.

_____ 11. A forecasting method using the opinions of outside experts

_____ 12. The planners' expectations with regard to the likely or probable state of events or conditions at some time in the future.

_____ 13. A model of a real or actual activity or process that behaves like the real activity or process.

_____ 14. A quantitative planning technique that attempts to determine the best way to allocate resources, when given possible alternative uses for and limitations on the resources.

_____ 15. A quantitative planning technique relating costs, revenue, and profit. It determines at what point income and expenses are equal.

_____ 16. A group of people who volunteer or are appointed to serve as investigators, problem solvers, or decision makers.

_____ 17. The overseeing of a project by a project manager who must plan, organize, staff, direct, and control those tasks needed to reach the desired outcomes.

_____ 18. Key people located throughout the organization who come together in an emergency to take charge and make the necessary decisions to deal with the impact on the organization.

BRAIN TEASERS

Write the answers to the following "brain teasers."

1. Discuss assumptions and forecasts. In your answer, define each and give its relationship to the planning process.

2. Differentiate between quantitative planning tools and general planning tools. In your answer, include a description and three examples of each category.

3. Discuss simulation and game theory. In your answer, include a definition of each. In addition, explain their similarities and differences.

4. Discuss worker participation techniques (quality circles) and brainstorming. In your answer, include a definition of each. In addition, explain their similarities, differences, and how a manager could utilize each.

RAPID REVIEW

Complete the following sentences with the appropriate words. The correct answers are located at the end of the chapter.

1. ________________ are the premises or conditions that planners accept as true or real, while ________________ are the expectations that planners formulate with regard to the likely or probable state of events or conditions some time in the future.
2. The two dilemmas faced by managers in trying to predict the future are ________________ and ________________.
3. Break-even analysis requires the manager to have information on ________________, ________________, and ________________.
4. ________ ________ is a planning tool used to predict competitive reactions.
5. Management by objectives is based upon the ________________ and the ________________ negotiating goals.

STUDENT EXERCISE

This exercise is designed to have you investigate a specific planning technique of a manager.

STEP 1. Interview the store manager of a large national/regional supermarket or discount store in your community. In interviewing, acquire the following information:

- How do you plan for the number of checkouts (registers) that will be open?
- What specific management planning techniques does your company provide for making this decision?
- Is the ratio of stations to customers determined by you or by company planners?
- What impact does the number of stations/waiting time have on your operating budget?

STEP 2. Summarize your findings in relation to the chapter material.

ANSWER KEY

ESSENTIAL TERMS

1. G	4. M	7. K	10. R	13. Q	16. E
2. O	5. I	8. D	11. H	14. L	17. N
3. A	6. B	9. P	12. J	15. C	18. F.

RAPID REVIEW

1. assumptions, forecasts
2. the constantly changing future and time
3. fixed costs, variable costs, and revenue
4. game theory
5. manager, employee

CHAPTER

6 Making Decisions

LEARNING OBJECTIVES

After reading and discussing this chapter, you should be able to:

1. Define this chapter's essential terms.
2. Recognize that decision making is a function of all managers at all levels.
3. Describe the formal decision-making process.
4. Explain the factors in the decision-making environment and the influences on decision making.
5. Discuss the importance of a manager's evaluating the effectiveness of a decision.
6. Discuss four decision-making aids.

OVERVIEW

WHAT IS DECISION MAKING?

Decision making is defined as a rational choice among alternatives. Decision making is universal: It is a part of all managers' jobs. A manager makes decisions constantly while performing the functions of planning, organizing, staffing, directing, and controlling. Because decision making is such an important element of a manager's job, it is necessary to utilize a conscious, rational decision-making process. A manager who makes decisions on a whim will not have the day-to-day decision-making success of the manager who consciously works through the decision-making process.

THE DECISION-MAKING PROCESS

The decision-making process is designed to solve a problem, which is the difference between what is and what should be. The decision-making process has seven steps. They are logical and simple in themselves, but they are all essential to the process.

DEFINE THE PROBLEM. Finding a solution to the problem will be greatly aided by properly identifying it. The consequences of not properly defining the problem are wasted time and energy. There is also the possibility of having to solve the "same" problem again. The accurate definition of a problem affects all other steps that follow. If a problem is inaccurately defined, every other step in the decision-making process will be based on that incorrect point.

IDENTIFY THE LIMITING OR CRITICAL FACTORS. Once the problem is defined, the manager needs to develop the limiting or critical factors of the problem. Limiting factors are those constraints that rule out certain alternative solutions. Time, resources, personnel, money, facilities, and equipment are common limiting factors.

DEVELOP POTENTIAL ALTERNATIVES. At this point it is necessary to look for, develop, and list as many possible alternatives—that is, solutions to the problem—as possible. These alternatives should eliminate, correct, or neutralize the problem. Sources for alternatives include past experience, other persons whose opinions and judgments are respected, and the practices of successful managers.

ANALYZE THE ALTERNATIVES. The purpose of this step is to decide on the relative merits of each of the alternatives. It is necessary to examine the positives and negatives of each alternative.

SELECT THE BEST ALTERNATIVE. In trying to select an alternative you must find the solution that appears to offer the fewest disadvantages and the most advantages. Sometimes the optimal solution is a combination of several of the alternatives.

IMPLEMENT THE SOLUTION. The solution needs effective implementation to yield the desired results. Everyone involved with the decision must know what he or she must do, how to do it, why and when. People must be sold on their roles and must know exactly what they must do and why. Programs, procedures, rules, or policies must be thoroughly put into effect.

ESTABLISH A CONTROL AND EVALUATION SYSTEM. Ongoing actions need to be monitored. The system should provide feedback on how well the decision was implemented, what the results are (positive or negative), and what adjustments are necessary to get the results that were wanted when the solution was chosen.

THE DECISION-MAKING ENVIRONMENT

A number of factors in the decision-making environment affect the process and the decision maker.

DEGREE OF CERTAINTY. There are three different decision-making environments. These environments require different responses from a manager. Decision making under conditions of certainty means that the manager has what is known as perfect knowledge. The manager has had this decision to make before, the alternatives are known, and the consequences of each alternative are fully understood. The manager will choose the alternative known to get the best results.

Decision making under conditions of risk provides a more difficult decision-making environment. In this situation the manager knows what the problem is and knows what the alternatives are, but does not know how each alternative will work out even though he or she knows the odds (probabilities) or possible outcomes. Finally, decision making under conditions of uncertainty is the most difficult for a manager. In this situation the manager is not able to determine the exact odds (probabilities) of the potential alternatives available.

DECISION STRATEGY: MAXIMIZING OR SATISFICING. All managers want to maximize their decisions: they want to make the best possible decisions. This requires ideal resources—information, time, personnel, equipment, and supplies. But managers operate in an environment that normally does not provide ideal resources. They do not always have the time to collect all the information they desire, so they choose to make the best decision possible with the information available and the time available—to satisfice.

INTERNAL ENVIRONMENT. A manager's decision-making environment is structured by superiors, subordinates, and organizational systems:

- Superiors can enhance or limit the decision-making effectiveness of a manager. A superior's confidence, security, and ability to delegate are aids to a supportive climate.
- Subordinates' support for, input to, and understanding of a decision are critical to a manager. The manager must evaluate the level of the subordinates' involvement, which can range from no input to full responsibility for decisions. Two factors influencing the necessary degree of subordinate involvement are the quality criteria (decisions that can be made by applying the formal decision-making process without considering the opinions of those affected), and the acceptance criteria (decisions requiring the understanding and support of those affected by it). A manager needs to examine a decision to determine which (or both) criteria are applicable to the situation.
- Organizational systems include the organization's policies, procedures, programs, and rules. These serve as boundaries for a manager's decision making.

EXTERNAL FORCES. In addition to dealing with the internal factors, a manager must consider external forces in the decision-making process. Customers, competitors, and government agencies are examples of external forces that cannot be controlled that can influence decisions.

INFLUENCES OF MANAGER'S STYLE

There are other influences on managerial decision making. Three of these influences are the manager's personal decision-making approach, the manager's ability to set priorities, and the timing of decisions.

PERSONAL DECISION-MAKING APPROACHES. Not all managers make decisions in the same way. There are three possible approaches:

- The rational/logical decision model proposes that the manager use a step-by-step process. It focuses on facts and logic while eliminating intuitive judgments.
- The nonrational/intuitive decision model relies on the manager's feelings about the situation. It is difficult to eliminate all elements of intuition from decision making, but the manager who relies on intuition for long-range decision making could be courting disaster.
- The predisposed decision model is illustrated by managers who decide on a solution, then gather evidence to support the decision. If a manager has this tendency, there is a strong possibility that he or she may ignore critical information.

ABILITY TO SET PRIORITIES. It is necessary to assign priorities to the making of decisions and to know your own reasons for the choices you make. Priorities can be established by determining which decision has the greatest impact on organizational goals, or by what the boss thinks, or based on likes or dislikes.

TIMING OF DECISIONS. After a decision is made it must be translated into action. Good timing plays an important part in successfully implementing a decision. Improper timing can harm the best decision.

AIDS TO DECISION MAKING

A manager has a number of strategies available to improve the quality of decisions. Each has a value when applied to the right situation.

INVOLVEMENT OF OTHERS. A manager can choose to involve others in the decision-making process, either through individual employee participation or through a structured committee. Involvement may result in utilizing insights and skills of others who may be better equipped than the manager to deal with elements of the decision. In addition this process will help to develop the talents of subordinates.

PROGRAMMING OF DECISIONS. Decisions that keep recurring can be quantified in routine decision-making steps or procedures. Typical business decisions that lend themselves to programming are summarizing company records, preparing company reports, handling routine correspondence, and preparing payrolls.

USING DECISION TREES. A decision tree is a pictorial representation of a potential decision. It allows the manager to show graphically which actions could be taken and how these actions relate to future events.

PAYBACK ANALYSIS. If a manager needs to evaluate capital purchasing alternatives, a sound strategy is to apply payback analysis. In this approach the manager ranks alternatives according to how long each would take to pay back its initial cost.

EVALUATING THE EFFECTIVENESS OF DECISIONS

Decisions and decision making are only as good as the results they achieve. The final step in the decision-making process is evaluation and control. This step is intended to provide feedback on the effectiveness of the decision as it is implemented. In addition, there are other devices and indicators of effectiveness. Accounting information and employee surveys will provide managers with control mechanisms while giving them a context within which to judge the decisions.

ESSENTIAL TERMS

Match the following essential terms with the proper definitions. The correct answers are located in the key at the end of the chapter.

A. alternative
B. decision
C. decision making
D. decision tree
E. limiting factors
F. maximize
G. payback analysis
H. problem
I. programmed decision
J. satisfice

____ 1. The difference between a desirable situation and what actually happens—the *what is* compared with the *what should be.*

____ 2. Make the best possible decision you can with the time and information you have available.

____ 3. A rational choice among alternatives—making a judgment or reaching a conclusion.

____ 4. The constraints managers work with that rule out potential alternatives.

____ 5. The result of making a judgment or reaching a conclusion.

____ 6. Resolution by routing decision-making steps or procedures of a recurring challenge or problem.

____ 7. Evaluation of investment alternatives by comparing the length of time necessary to pay back their initial costs.

____ 8. A potential course of action that is likely to

eliminate, correct, or neutralize the cause of a problem.

_____ 9. A graphic representation of the actions a manager can take and how these actions relate to future events.

_____ 10. Make the best possible decision. Requires ideal resources—information, time, personnel, equipment, and supplies.

BRAIN TEASERS

Write the answers to the following "brain teasers."

1. Discuss what is meant by the statement "decision making is universal among management positions." Provide examples.

2. Discuss the decision-making process. In your answer, list the decision-making steps and give an explanation of each step.

3. Discuss the decision-making environment. In your answer, explain the four components and give an example of each.

4. Discuss the influences of a manager's style on decision making. In your answer, explain the three influences and give an example of each.

5. Discuss the aids to decision making. In your answer, explain the four aids and give an example of the application of each one.

6. Answer the following question: "How may a manager evaluate the effectiveness of decisions?"

RAPID REVIEW

Complete the following sentences with the appropriate words. The correct answers are located in the key at the end of the chapter.

1. A manager makes decisions under conditions of ____________, ____________, and ____________.
2. A strategy in which a manager makes the best decision possible within the ____________ and with the ____________ is known as ____________.
3. A decision model in which the manager makes a decision, then collects information to justify it is known as the ____________ model.
4. When to implement a decision is known as ____________.
5. ______ ______ is a decision aid used to evaluate capital purchasing alternatives.

STUDENT EXERCISE

This exercise is designed for you to make management decisions.

STEP 1. Read the following scenario.

It is Tuesday afternoon. You have been gone from work all morning at meetings and have just arrived at your office. When you enter you are greeted by the following situations:

____ A preliminary report of test results on the new product has just been delivered. The lab cannot proceed with further tests until you respond to this report. The anticipated time: 30 minutes.

____ A telegram from your salesperson in Chicago requests approval for priority processing of a large order. Anticipated time: 15 minutes.

____ A note from your boss says he wants to see you as soon as you arrive. You know he always takes 30 to 60 minutes regardless of the topic.

____ Your telephone is ringing. It may be Chicago.

____ Your production foreman wants to talk to you immediately. She heard about plans for a work slow down to begin tonight on the third shift. Estimated time: 60 minutes minimum.

____ A note from a peer manager requests 15 minutes of your time as soon as possible to discuss something of vital concern to both of you. His note does not specify what the topic is.

____ Your secretary became ill at lunch and left word that she is resting in the company infirmary. It will take 10 minutes to check on her.

____ Three persons are seated in your outer office. Two appear to be sales persons and one a job applicant. It will take 10 minutes just to find out who they are.

____ You just remembered a purchase order that has to be processed today to keep your production schedule on target. Estimated time: 15 minutes.

STEP 2. Prioritize the events in the order you would solve them. The first situation to be resolved would be number one and the last would be number nine.

STEP 3. Explain why you established these priorities.

ANSWER KEY

ESSENTIAL TERMS

1. H	3. C	5. B	7. G	9. D
2. J	4. E	6. I	8. A	10. F

RAPID REVIEW

1. certainty, risk, and uncertainty
2. time, information available, satisficing
3. predisposed
4. timing
5. payback analysis

CHAPTER

7 Organizing: The Formal Organization

LEARNING OBJECTIVES

After reading and discussing this chapter, you should be able to:

1. Define this chapter's essential terms.
2. Explain the relationship between the management functions of planning and organizing.
3. Explain the importance of the organizing process.
4. List and discuss the five steps in the organizing process.
5. Describe and give an example of the five kinds of approaches to organizing.
6. Discuss the concept of authority, its sources, and its types.
7. Explain the concept of power and its sources.
8. Discuss the following concepts as they apply to organizations:
    - Unity of command
    - Span of control
    - Centralization vs. decentralization
    - Delegation

OVERVIEW

ORGANIZING DEFINED

Organizing is the management function that establishes relationships between activity and authority. The end result of an organizing process is an organization—a whole consisting of unified parts (a system) acting in harmony to execute tasks to achieve goals effectively and efficiently.

THE RELATIONSHIP BETWEEN PLANNING AND ORGANIZING. The managerial functions of planning and organizing are intimately related. Organizing begins with and is governed by plans; and plans state where the organization is going and how it will get there. An organization must be built or an existing one modified, to see to it that plans are executed and that goals are reached. The organization structure should be responsive to changes in plans.

IMPORTANCE OF THE ORGANIZING PROCESS. Management is very much interested in the successful completion of the organizing process. It is also concerned with the subsequent development, or modification, of an organization's structure. The organizing process will make it possible to attain the purpose of the organization. It also should provide:

- A clarified work environment. Everyone should know what to do. Tasks, responsibilities, and types and limits of authority will have been determined.
- A coordinated environment. Confusion should be minimized and obstacles to performance removed. The interrelationship of the various work units will have been developed. Guidelines for interaction among personnel will have been developed. In addition, the principle of unity of direction should be achieved: This principle calls for the establishment of one authority figure for each designated task of the organization—this person has the authority to coordinate all plans concerning the task.
- A formal decision-making structure. Through the organization chart, the formal superior–subordinate relationships have been developed. This allows an orderly progression up through the hierarchy for decision making and decision-making communication.

THE ORGANIZING PROCESS

By applying the organizing process, management will improve the possibilities of achieving a functioning work environment. Organizing consists of a five-step process.

STEP 1. Consider plans and goals. Plans and their goals affect organizing and its result—the organization. Plans dictate the purposes and activities that organizations have or will have. As the plans and activities of the organization change, the organization structure will respond.

STEP 2. Determine the work activities necessary to accomplish objectives. What work activities are necessary to accomplish the identified organizational objectives? Creating a list of tasks to be accomplished begins with those that will be ongoing tasks and ends with the unique, or one-time-only tasks. Hiring, training, and record keeping are part of the regular routine for running any business. In addition, it is necessary to identify the unique needs of the organization.

STEP 3. Classify and group activities. This step asks managers to perform three processes:

- Examine each activity to determine its general nature (marketing, production, finance, personnel, etc.).
- Group the activities into these related areas (division of labor).
- Establish the basic department design for the organization structure (departmentation).

STEP 4. Assign work and delegate appropriate authority. The activities now must be assigned to individuals who are simultaneously given the appropriate authority to accomplish the task. The guiding concept in this step is the principle of functional definition—in establishing departments, the nature, purpose, tasks and performance of the department must first be determined as a basis for authority. The activities determine the type and quantity of authority necessary.

STEP 5. Design a hierarchy of relationships. This step requires the determination of both vertical and horizontal operating relationships of the organization as a whole. The vertical structuring of the organization results in a decision-making hierarchy that shows who is in charge of each task, of each specialty area, and of the organization as a whole. The horizontal structuring has two important effects: It defines the working relationships between operating departments, and it makes the final decision on the span of control (the number of subordinates under the direction) of each manager.

The result of this is a complete organization structure. The structure is shown visibly by an organization chart. An organization chart shows:

- Who reports to whom—the chain of command.
- How many subordinates work for each manager—the span of control.
- Channels of official communication through the solid lines that connect each job.
- How the company is structured—by function, customer, or product, for example.
- The work being done in each job—the labels on the boxes.
- The hierarchy of decision making—where a decision maker for a problem is located.
- How current the present organization structure is (if a date is on the chart).
- Types of authority relationships—solid connections between boxes illustrate line authority, and dotted lines show staff and functional authority.

APPROACHES TO ORGANIZING

Whatever the organization's approach to its structural design, it should represent the most effective and efficient use for all resources. Five options are available.

THE FUNCTIONAL APPROACH. Probably the most common approach to organizing is the functional approach. It groups activities under the major headings that nearly every business has in common—finance, production, marketing, and personnel. These are the functions of the business, and the entire organization would be divided into these major areas. It is a logical way to organize for most businesses. It avoids overlap in the execution of basic business activities. Difficulties can arise with this format. Because employees are separated from one another, their understanding and concern for specialty areas other than their own is not easy to achieve. This can lead to communication problems and lack of cooperation. In addition, the functional pattern does not develop generalists.

THE GEOGRAPHIC APPROACH. Grouping activities for one department, or for an enterprise, under geographic heads or territories makes sense in various marketing, financial, and production companies. Geographic patterns work best when different laws, currencies, languages, and traditions exist, and have a direct impact on the ways in which business activities must be conducted. In addition, the geographic structure furnishes a training ground to develop general management capabilities. Better coordination for the activities in the geographic area is also a positive result of this approach. A limitation of this format is the cost of personnel and facilities. When a company decides to expand geographically, it automatically incurs costs through duplication of personnel positions and additional office sites.

THE PRODUCT LINE APPROACH. The establishment of an organization pattern based on product should be considered when attention, energy, and efforts need to be focused on an organization's particular products. It can create healthy organizational competition. The major disadvantage is similar to that of the geographical structure—cost through duplication of business functions within each product line.

THE CUSTOMER APPROACH. Organizing around groups of customers makes economic sense when the customers are distinct enough in their demands, preferences, and needs to justify it. Just how far an organization should carry the customer approach depends on internal decisions about how best to serve itself and its customers, patients, or clients. If the decision is made to use this approach with only some of a firm's customers, there will be difficulty in coordinating the customer-based department with departments organized on other patterns. Another possibility is overspecialization: the facilities and personnel may become so keyed to solving the needs of their customers that they cannot be used for any other purpose—resulting in underutilization.

THE MATRIX APPROACH. A matrix organization pattern is a design blending the functional organization structure with a project team structure. The matrix approach utilizes the technical resources of an organization by efficiently allocating expertise where and when it is needed. It should produce a coordinated project, thus minimizing conflicting specialty areas. Project participation places a premium on interpersonal skills.

MAJOR ORGANIZATIONAL CONCEPTS

It is necessary to be familiar with some major organizational concepts and principles that managers work with in developing a workable system. A working knowledge of authority, power, delegation, span of control, and the centralization vs. decentralization issue are essential.

AUTHORITY: THE CONCEPT AND APPLICATION. Authority is a management tool. It can be described as the right to commit resources (that is, to make decisions that commit an organization's resources), or the legal (legitimate) right to give orders (to tell someone to do or not to do something). A manager gains his authority through two sources: the formal authority granted in a job description, and the willingness of employees to accept the manager's legitimate authority.

While authority is positional—it will be there when the incumbent leaves—power is personal. Power exists because of the person. Power is the ability to exert influence in the organization. The sources of power are:

- Legitimate or position power.
- Power to reward or punish.
- Referent or charismatic power.
- Expert power.

In an organization, different types of authority are created by the relationships between individuals and between departments. There are three types of authority:

- Line authority is direct supervisory authority.
- Staff authority is advisory in nature.
- Functional authority is authority delegated to an individual or department over specific activities undertaken by personnel in other departments.

A concept often confused with line and staff authority is the concept of line and staff departments. A line department is established to meet the major objectives of the company. A staff department assists in meeting the objectives.

A concern of all managers in the application of both staff and functional authority is the violation of the principle of unity of command: this principle means that each person in the organization should take orders from and report to only one boss. While this is an ideal situation it may not always be possible.

DELEGATION. Delegation is a concept describing the passing ot formal authority to another person. The application of the concept is done through a series of events:

- Assignment of tasks. Specific tasks are identified by the supervisor.
- Delegation of authority. The authority necessary to do the task is determined.
- Acceptance of responsibility. Responsibility is the obligation to carry out one's assigned duties to the best of one's ability. Responsibility is not delegated by a manager to an employee, but the employee becomes obligated when the assignment is accepted.
- Creation of accountability. Accountability is having to answer to someone for your actions. When the subordinate accepts the assignment and the authority, he or she will be held accountable or answerable for actions taken.

SPAN OF CONTROL. The span of control or span of management is the number of subordinates each manager should have to direct. The exact number is determined by an interplay of four variables: the complexity and variety of the subordinates' work; the ability and training of the subordinates themselves; the ability of the managers; and the company philosophy for centralization or decentralization of decision making.

CENTRALIZATION VS. DECENTRALIZATION. The terms centralization and decentralization refer to a philosophy of organization and management that focuses on either the selective concentration (centralization) or the dispersal (decentralization) of authority within an organization structure. The question of where authority rests is resolved in an operating philosophy of management—either to concentrate authority for decision making in the hands of a few, or to force it down the organization structure into the hands of many. There are guidelines to follow in determining the degree of decentralization in a company:

- The greater the number of decisions made at lower levels of management, the more the company is decentralized.
- The more important the decisions made at lower levels, the greater is decentralization.
- The more flexible the interpretation of company policy at the lower levels, the greater is the degree of decentralization.
- The more widely dispersed the operations of the company geographically, the greater is the degree of decentralization.
- The less a subordinate has to refer to his or her manager prior to a decision, the greater is the decentralization.

The company's philosophy of centralization or decentralization can influence the span of control. A philosophy of decentralized decision making generally means the span of control should be wider for each manager. Conversely, a philosophy of centralized decision making should result in a narrower span of control.

ESSENTIAL TERMS

Match the following essential terms with the proper definitions. The correct answers are located in the key at the end of the chapter.

A. accountability
B. authority
C. chain of command
D. delegation
E. departmentation
F. division of labor
G. functional authority
H. line authority
I. line departments
J. organization
K. organization chart
L. organizing
M. power
N. responsibility
O. span of control
P. staff authority
Q. staff departments
R. unity of command
S. unity of direction

____ 1. The right to make decisions that commit the organization's resources or the legal right to tell someone to do or not to do something.

____ 2. The principle of organization that is concerned with the number of subordinates each manager should have to direct.

____ 3. The study of tasks deemed essential, the breaking down of tasks into parts or steps, and the assigning of one or more of those parts to an individual.

____ 4. The result of the organizing process.

____ 5. A person's ability to influence results.

____ 6. The organization principle that states that each group of activities having the same objective should have one head.

____ 7. Being answerable for one's actions.

____ 8. Authority to serve in an advisory capacity; authority to advise.

____ 9. The downward transfer of

formal authority from one person to another.

_____ 10. A visual representation of the way in which an entire organization and each of its parts fit together.

_____ 11. The organizing principle that states that each person in an organization should take orders from and report to only one person.

_____ 12. The organizing principle concerned with the number of management positions in an organization and their unbroken connection to its top position.

_____ 13. Direct supervisory authority from superior to subordinate.

_____ 14. The obligation to carry out one's assigned duties to the best of one's ability.

_____ 15. These assist line departments in meeting the objectives of the organization through advice or technical assistance.

_____ 16. The management activity that determines the work activities to be done, classifies and groups that work, assigns the activities and delegates authority to do the work, and designs a hierarchy of decision-making relationships.

_____ 17. Authority over specific activities that are undertaken by personnel in other departments.

_____ 18. The creation of groups, subdivisions, or departments that will execute and oversee the various tasks that management considers essential.

_____ 19. Departments established to meet the major objectives of the organization.

BRAIN TEASERS

Write the answers to the following "brain teasers."

1. Discuss the importance of organizing. Include in your answer a discussion of the relationship of planning and organizing as well as three positive results of organizing.

2. Discuss the organizing process. In developing your answer list and explain each of the five steps in the process.

3. Discuss the approaches to organizing. In developing your answer describe each of the five potential approaches, and the advantages and disadvantages of each.

4. Discuss authority and power. In your answer include a definition of each, sources of each, and types of authority.

5. Discuss the concept of delegation. In your answer include a definition of delegation and an explanation of the four-step process involved.

6. Discuss span of control. Include in your answer the definition of span of control and an explanation of the four variables that influence span of control.

7. Discuss the concepts of centralization and decentralization. Include in your answer a definition of each and an explanation of how each is applied.

RAPID REVIEW

Complete the following sentences with the appropriate words. The correct answers are located in the key at the end of the chapter.

1. ____________ authority is direct supervisory authority.
2. The downward transfer of authority from one person to another is known as ____________.
3. ____________ can be delegated while ____________ is an obligation and cannot be delegated.
4. The ____________ is influenced by the amount of training employees have had.
5. Authority over specific activities that are undertaken by personnel in other departments is known as ______ ______.

STUDENT EXERCISE

This exercise is designed to have you establish an organization.

STEP 1. Read the list below of activities being performed in the U. R. Grate Company.

- machining
- selling
- hiring
- record keeping
- shipping
- training
- assembling
- advertising
- auditing
- pricing
- compensating
- painting

STEP 2. Develop an organization structure based on a function pattern. U. R. Grate, president, wants:

- only four major functional departments
- not more than three for a span of control for each department head
- all hiring practices to be uniform, even though all managers may hire their own employees.

ANSWER KEY

ESSENTIAL TERMS

1. B	5. M	9. D	13. H	17. G
2. O	6. S	10. K	14. N	18. E
3. F	7. A	11. R	15. Q	19. I
4. J	8. P	12. C	16. L	

RAPID REVIEW

1. line
2. delegation
3. authority, responsibility
4. span of control
5. functional authority

CHAPTER

8 Organizing: The Informal Organization

LEARNING OBJECTIVES

After reading and discussing this chapter, you should be able to:

1. Define this chapter's essential terms.
2. Explain the importance of a manager's recognizing and working with the informal organization.
3. Explain what is meant by informal organization.
4. Discuss three types of informal groups characteristic of the informal organization.
5. Explain why people form informal groups and why the groups stay in existence.
6. Explain the basis of leadership within the informal organization.
7. Discuss two important characteristics of informal groups.
8. Describe the positive and negative impact of the informal organization on the formal organization.
9. Discuss strategies managers can use to work with the informal organization.

OVERVIEW

THE INFORMAL ORGANIZATION DEFINED

The informal organization is a network of personal and social relationships that arises spontaneously as people associate with one another in a work environment. It is composed of all the informal groupings of people within a formal organization. The informal organization presents a challenge for a manager because it consists of actual operating relationships not prescribed by the formal organization and, therefore, not shown on the company's organization chart.

TYPES OF GROUPS IN THE INFORMAL ORGANIZATION

Informal groups may be described as horizontal, vertical, or mixed. These titles identify the composition of the group by the levels of its members within the formal organization and by the similarity or dissimilarity of their work assignments. Let's examine each.

HORIZONTAL GROUPS. Horizontal groups include persons who are on the same level of the organization. These groups can consist of the members in the same work area or can have membership across department lines.

VERTICAL GROUPS. Vertical groups include people on different levels of the formal organization. These people always come together within the same work areas. A vertical group can consist of a supervisor and one or more of his or her employees. It may also be formed through skip-level relationships—a top-level manager may associate with a first-level manager.

MIXED GROUPS. A mixed group consists of people whose positions are on different levels of the formal organization and in different work areas. An example is provided by a vice president who develops a close relationship with the director of computer services in order to get preferential treatment.

FUNCTIONS OF THE INFORMAL ORGANIZATION

Why do individuals form informal groups? Why do these groups remain in existence? These questions are of concern to managers.

WHY PEOPLE FORM INFORMAL GROUPS. Informal groups are formed for different reasons.

- They provide the opportunity to satisfy needs.
- They arise because people work near one another.
- They provide the opportunity for people to associate with others with whom they have something in common (attitudes, beliefs, personality, sex, race, economic position, perceived abilities).

WHY INFORMAL GROUPS REMAIN IN EXISTENCE. Informal groups remain in existence because they serve four major functions.

- They maintain the social and cultural values the group members hold in common.
- They provide members the opportunity for status and the opportunity for social interaction and fulfillment.
- They provide information for members.
- They influence the work environment.

STRUCTURE OF THE INFORMAL ORGANIZATION

In informal groups, leaders emerge and member roles evolve.

LEADERSHIP OF THE GROUP. Leaders of informal groups arise for various reasons: age, seniority, charisma, work location, technical ability, or the opportunity to move around the work area freely. There is a possibility that the group may have several leaders of varying importance who perform different functions. One person may be an expert on organization matters, another on social matters, and a third on technical questions.

NON-LEADER ROLES FOR MEMBERS. Normally in an informal group there is an inner core or primary group; a fringe group, which functions in and out of the group; and an out-status group, which though identified with the group does not actively participate. There are two tools that managers can use to identify the existence of informal groups and their composition. One tool is a sociogram (a diagram of group attraction). The other is an interaction chart (a diagram that shows the informal interactions people have with one another).

UTILIZING GROUP ROLES. Recognizing that informal groups exist is step one for a manager. The second step is identifying the roles members play within the group. And the third step is having the intelligence to use this information to work with the informal group. A manager works with a group or groups of employees who have a personality, values, and a culture. Managers need to be able to identify the leaders of these groups and work with them to influence the total group. It is not logical to try to influence a group by appealing to a fringe member. The leaders are at the core of decision making.

SIGNIFICANT CHARACTERISTICS OF INFORMAL ORGANIZATIONS

Informal organizations develop two identifiable characteristics: norms and cohesion.

DEVELOPMENT OF NORMS. Norms are standards of behavior that are accepted by all group members. A norm serves as a guideline. It tells group members what they can or cannot do under certain circumstances. Once norms are established and agreed upon by the group, they act as an internal control device on members.

DEVELOPMENT OF COHESION. Cohesion is measured by the degree to which members share the group's goals and cooperate with one another. Cohesiveness is an indication of how much control the group has over its members—the more cohesion, the more control.

IMPACT OF THE INFORMAL ORGANIZATION

The groups that compose the informal organization can affect the formal organization negatively and positively.

NEGATIVE IMPACT. There are four potential problem areas associated with the informal organization:

- Resistance to change. In an effort to protect its values and beliefs, the informal group can place roadblocks in the path to any modifications in the work environment.
- Conflict. The informal group can create two masters for an employee. In an attempt to satisfy the informal group, the employee may come in conflict with the formal organization.
- Rumor. The informal communication system—the grapevine—can create or process false information or rumors.
- Pressure to conform. The norms that the informal group develops act as strong inducement toward conformity. The more cohesive the group, the more accepted are the behavioral standards.

POSITIVE IMPACT. The informal group can be helpful to managers. It has five potential benefits.

- It makes the total system effective. If the informal organization blends well with the formal system, the organization can function more effectively.
- It supports management. It can fill in gaps in the manager's knowledge through advice or through performing the work—for example in budgeting and scheduling.
- It provides stability in the environment. The informal organization can provide acceptance and belonging. It can also provide a place to vent frustrations.
- It provides a useful communications channel. It provides employees with the opportunity to exchange social information, to discuss their work, and to understand what is happening in the work environment.
- It encourages better management. Planned changes by managers should be made with an awareness of the ability of the informal group to make the plan succeed or fail.

INFORMAL COMMUNICATION—THE GRAPEVINE

The informal communication system in an organization is known as the grapevine. It is an important part of the organizational environment. What are its causes, characteristics, patterns, and problems?

WHY DOES THE GRAPEVINE OCCUR? The grapevine is the result of social interaction in an organization. People talk about their work, their frustrations, and their successes. The activity on the grapevine is a result more of the situation in the work environment than of the natural inclination of the person. Environmental factors leading to participation include feelings of high anxiety and insecurity, familiarity with the subject, the possession of new information, and access to information.

CHARACTERISTICS OF GRAPEVINES. A grapevine is fast and it can penetrate the tightest security. In addition, the grapevine is easily accessible.

PATTERNS OF GRAPEVINES. There are four grapevine patterns (single chain, cluster chain, gossip, and random). The most common pattern is the cluster chain.

PROBLEMS THE GRAPEVINE CAN CAUSE. There are two problems associated with the grapevine. One is that it is not totally accurate. There is a tendency to omit some major pieces of information that have a bearing on accuracy. A second problem is rumor. Rumor is information that is communicated without evidence of truth.

STRATEGIES FOR WORKING WITH THE INFORMAL ORGANIZATION

Every manager experiences the effects of the informal organization. Successful managers learn that the informal organization has benefits when managed correctly. In order to do this the manager should:

- Start strategy development with a recognition of and acceptance of the existence of the informal organization.
- Identify the informal groups and who leads them.
- Develop strategies to align the informal organization's goals and activities with those of the formal organization.

ESSENTIAL TERMS

Match the following essential terms with the proper definitions. The correct answers are located in the key at the end of the chapter.

A. cohesion
B. grapevine
C. horizontal group
D. informal organization
E. interaction chart
F. mixed group
G. norm
H. sociogram
I. vertical group

_____ 1. A diagram that shows the informal interactions people have with one another.

_____ 2. A diagram of group attraction.

_____ 3. The measure of a group's solidarity—the degree to which the members share resources and ideas and the degree of their willingness to cooperate with one another.

_____ 4. An informal group composed of persons in different work areas and in different levels of the formal organization.

_____ 5. An informal group composed of individuals within the same work areas or on the same level of the formal organization.

_____ 6. An informal group composed of individuals who work in the same work areas but on different levels of the formal organization.

_____ 7. Any standard of conduct, code, or pattern of behavior perceived by a group to be important for its members to honor or to conform to.

_____ 8. The communication system of the informal organization. It carries both rumors and messages.

_____ 9. The collection and interaction of informal groups within the formal organization.

BRAIN TEASERS

Write the answers to the following "brain teasers."

1. Discuss the informal organization. Include in your discussion a definition and a description of the three groups that compose the informal organization.

2. Discuss the functions of the informal organization. In your answer, include the reasons why informal groups occur and why they remain in existence.

3. Discuss informal organization leadership. Include in your answer the leader–member roles, how leadership is decided upon, and multiple leadership possibilities.

4. Discuss the four *negative* effects the informal organization has on the formal organization.

5. Discuss the five *positive* effects the informal organization has on the formal organization.

6. Discuss the grapevine. Include in your discussion why it occurs, its characteristics, its patterns, and its potential problems.

7. Write a memorandum to your boss entitled "Strategies for Working with the Informal Organization."

RAPID REVIEW

Complete the following sentences with the appropriate words. The correct answers are located in the key at the end of the chapter.

1. The three types of groups in the informal organization are ________, ________, and ________.
2. ________ is a measure of a group's solidarity.
3. A ________ is a standard, or code, or pattern of behavior perceived by a group to be important for its members to honor or to conform to.
4. People form informal groups because of needs, ________, and ________.
5. The common patterns for the grapevine are ________, ________, ________, and ________.

STUDENT EXERCISE

Examine your experiences with the informal organization and informal groups.

STEP 1. Develop a list of groups in which you have been or are now involved (church, hobby, sports, work).

STEP 2. For each group, answer the following questions.

- Who was the person everyone recognized as the informal leader?
- Why was this person recognized?
- Was it always the same person?
- Were there groups within the group? If so, why?
- If sub-groups existed, were they positive or negative? Give examples.

STEP 3. Summarize your findings in relation to the chapter material.

ANSWER KEY

ESSENTIAL TERMS

1. E	3. A	5. C	7. G	9. D
2. H	4. F	6. I	8. B	

RAPID REVIEW

1. horizontal, vertical, mixed
2. cohesion
3. norm
4. proximity, similarity
5. single chain, gossip, random, cluster chain

CHAPTER

9 Staffing

LEARNING OBJECTIVES

After reading and discussing this chapter, you should be able to:

1. Define this chapter's essential terms.
2. Explain the importance of the staffing function and its relationship to planning and organizing.
3. List and describe the steps in the staffing process.
4. Explain the impact of equal employment opportunity and affirmative action on the staffing process.
5. Discuss the human resource planning process.
6. Outline the selection process, and describe each of the steps.
7. Distinguish between induction and orientation.
8. Define and distinguish between training and development.
9. Discuss the purposes and types of performance appraisal.

OVERVIEW

THE RIGHT PERSON IN THE RIGHT JOB

In order to survive and prosper, an organization must be able to identify, select, develop, and retain qualified personnel. People are the most important resource of an organization. They supply the talent, skills, knowledge, and experience to achieve the organization's objectives. The challenge for management is to match personnel with the jobs identified and developed during the organizing process.

STAFFING DEFINED

The staffing function can be viewed as consisting of a series of steps that managers perform in order to provide the organization with the right people in the right positions. The eight steps in the process are:

1. Human resource planning.
2. Recruitment.
3. Selection.
4. Induction and orientation.
5. Training and development.
6. Performance appraisal.
7. Employment decisions.
8. Separations.

THE LEGAL ENVIRONMENT OF STAFFING

The staffing process of an organization is influenced by the legal environment. Major legislation has been enacted to provide for an employment environment in which both job applicants and present employees are free from discrimination in their pursuit of employment opportunities. In addition, legislation encourages employers to actively resolve the results of past discrimination by developing affirmative action plans.

EQUAL EMPLOYMENT OPPORTUNITY. Employment choices made on the basis of race, color, religion, sex, age, or national origin are prohibited. It is unlawful for an employer to do either of the following:

- To fail or refuse to hire or to discharge an individual because of race, color, religion, sex, age, or national origin.
- To limit, segregate, or classify his or her employees or applicants for employment in any way that would tend to deprive individuals of employment opportunities because of race, color, religion, sex, age, or national origin.

The purpose of the legislation is to prevent discrimination that is overt (purposely not hiring or advancing) and covert (resulting from employment procedures, not of intentional practice). An example of overt discrimination would be a manager stating that he wants "a man for the job, not a woman," when either could do the job equally well. Covert discrimination may occur within the employment system. A test that results in minority groups failing in a much greater percentage than whites is racially discriminatory if the test is not job-related. This is also an example of adverse impact (any part of the employment process that results in a significantly higher percentage of a protected group being rejected for employment than of a nonprotected group).

AFFIRMATIVE ACTION. Affirmative action goes beyond equal employment opportunity. It requires an employer to make an extra effort to hire and promote those in a protected minority. The purpose of affirmative action is to eliminate the present effects of past discrimination.

HUMAN RESOURCE PLANNING

The overall human resource planning process for an organization involves forecasting the demand for and supply of personnel. There are three elements to the planning: forecasting personnel requirements, comparing requirements to the inventory of potential candidates within the organization, and planning for how many people to recruit or who to train.

HUMAN RESOURCE FORECASTING. Human resource forecasting attempts to predict the organization's future demands for people and jobs. In forecasting personnel requirements, management needs to consider the strategic plans of the organization and the normal employee turnover. Strategic plans determine the direction of the company and its need for people. These statistics are, in turn, modified by figures on employee turnover. The number of retirements, resignations, and terminations also needs to be included with the initial forecast.

HUMAN RESOURCE INVENTORY. The human resource inventory provides information about the organization's present personnel. After the inventory is completed, an organization will have catalogued the skills, abilities, interests, and needs of the work force. Management will know who occupies each position, as well as his or her qualifications, length of service, and responsibilities.

COMPARISON OF FORECAST AND INVENTORY. Once the personnel forecast is completed and the personnel inventory has been finalized, a comparison is made to determine the answers to these questions:

- Do present employees possess the necessary prerequisites? If so, should they be considered?
- If they do not possess the skills, can the skills be provided through training?
- If the existing employees do not have the skills, where can persons with these skills be located outside the company?

ROLE OF THE INDIVIDUAL MANAGER. Regardless of whether or not the organization has the services of human resource planners, individual managers need to be actively involved in the human resource planning process. The involvement is both in determining the need for additional or replacement personnel and in negotiating the approval of the position with his or her manager.

RECRUITMENT

In recruitment the organization attempts to identify and attract candidates to meet the requirements of anticipated or actual position vacancies. Two devices used during this phase to aid the proper identification of candidates are a job description (demands of the job) and job specifications (qualifications needed to perform the job).

SOURCES OF APPLICANTS. There are two sources of applicants—internal and external.

Internal applicants are recruited from referrals made by friends and relatives in the organization, through company newsletters, and by searching through performance records of present employees. Internal recruiting can reduce turnover, provide incentive to learn jobs quickly, and assist in making the individual a functioning member of the organization faster because the person already knows the policies and expectations of the company. There are two potential drawbacks: employees who do not get the job may become disinterested, and the practice of internal recruiting can result in minimal "new blood" being brought into the organization.

External applicants are recruited using on-site visits to colleges, trade schools, professional conferences, trade fairs, and high schools. Another tactic is to place advertisements in newspapers and trade journals or to place job requisitions with unions, school placement bureaus, and private or public employment agencies. Limitations on using outside sources include cost and job vacancy being recruited for.

ROLE OF THE INDIVIDUAL MANAGER. A manager may have two roles in the recruitment process. For internal sources, the manager may be asked to identify potential candidates for openings in the organization on the basis of their performance while in the manager's department. For external sources, the line manager is often asked to participate in recruiting trips to colleges, trade fairs, or professional association meetings.

SELECTION

Selection is the process of deciding which candidate, out of the pool of applicants developed in recruitment has the abilities, skills, and characteristics most closely matching job demands. The decision comes after the candidates go through a series of steps that compose the selection process.

THE SELECTION PROCESS. The selection process is composed of seven steps. They are:

1. THE APPLICATION BLANK. Prospective employees are requested to complete an application blank. This provides applicant information on education, experience, growth, and employment stability.

2. PRELIMINARY INTERVIEW. This step attempts to screen out the obviously unqualified.

3. TESTING. The purpose of employment testing is to determine the candidate's ability to perform the job. Potential tests include aptitude tests (person's ability to learn concepts), performance tests (what a person can do at the time of testing), and personality tests (individual characteristics, traits, and motivations).

4. IN-DEPTH INTERVIEWS. The in-depth interview will provide the applicant's prospective manager or managers the opportunity to verify information on hand and to find out more about the applicant's interests, as-

pirations, and expectations. It also provides the opportunity to share information on the company, the job, and environmental conditions.

5. REFERENCE CHECKS. Applicants are normally asked to supply personal or work references on the application blank. Personal references—clergy, doctors, friends—are of little value to an employer because applicants do not normally list people who will provide negative information. Work references, on the other hand, have value provided the reference feels free to communicate.

6. PHYSICAL EXAMINATIONS. Prior to tendering a job offer, some organizations require potential candidates to take a physical examination. The purposes are:

- To prevent insurance claims for illnesses or injuries that occurred prior to employment by the company.
- To detect any communicable diseases.
- To certify that the person is physically capable of performing the job.

7. OFFER OF EMPLOYMENT. At this point, the top-ranking applicant is offered a job by management. This may involve a series of negotiations on initial salary, depending on the organization's compensation philosophy.

ROLE OF THE INDIVIDUAL MANAGER. The individual manager should be actively involved in the selection process. If the initial screening is not performed by the prospective applicant's manager, the in-depth interview will be. After the interviews the manager's further role in selection will be determined by the company's philosophy, size, degree of specialization, and the manager's ability.

INDUCTION AND ORIENTATION

When an employee is hired, two processes are started—induction and orientation. The immediate goal of these processes is to bring the employee into the mainstream of the organization as quickly as possible.

INDUCTION. The purpose of induction is to provide the new employee with necessary information about the company. It familiarizes the new person with the duties and benefits of employment, company history, its products or services, and the organization structure. Induction is accomplished through an interaction of the employee, the immediate supervisor, and the personnel specialist.

ORIENTATION. The purpose of orientation is to have the new employee become oriented to the working environment and operating reality. The employee and manager will discuss specifics of the work—location, rules, equipment, procedures, and plans for training. In addition, the employee and manager have the opportunity to discuss and reinforce performance expectations that were initially discussed during the interview process. The new employee may be paired with an experienced employee for a period of time to help the socialization process.

TRAINING AND DEVELOPMENT

Training and development programs in organizations have different goals. In addition, they utilize different techniques.

TRAINING: PURPOSES AND TECHNIQUES. Training supplies skills, knowledge, and attitudes needed by individuals or groups to improve their abilities to perform their present jobs. Training is used to give employees skills or to brush up existing skills to the level necessary to perform the job. As jobs change or as an employee demonstrates the need for additional skills, the organization provides more training.

Various training techniques can be employed by management. A person can be trained off the job in a classroom setting, or on the job (OJT), or using a simulated work environment (vestibule training). Regardless of the type, training should be realistic, designed with the trainee in mind, and should be conducted by people who know the material to be taught, know how to train, and want to conduct training.

DEVELOPMENT: PURPOSES AND TECHNIQUES. Development programs get people ready for their and the organization's futures. Development usually takes place outside the immediate company environment and is often conducted by outside professionals. Development exposes people to skills, knowledge, and attitudes that will be helpful in higher positions. In addition to seminars, workshops, college tuition refund programs, and leaves of absence for pursuit of advanced degrees, companies may utilize job rotation, internships, apprenticeships, or assisantships for development purposes.

PERFORMANCE APPRAISAL

Performance appraisal is a formal, structured system designed to measure the actual job performance of an employee compared to designated performance standards. A manager should use appraisal to accomplish certain definite objectives:

1. Develop individual plans for improvement based on agreed-upon goals, strengths, and weaknesses.
2. Identify growth opportunities.
3. Document present job performance to provide superiors with information to make decisions on salary, promotion, demotion, and termination.
4. Provide the opportunity for formal feedback.

WHAT ARE THE FACTORS IN SUCCESSFUL APPRAISALS? The success of performance appraisal is a function of the parties involved and the systems used. The manager and subordinate must be aware of the purposes behind a performance appraisal and they must have faith in the process and the instruments it uses. Each must take the time to prepare for the session. Each party must understand the appraisal system to be used and what criteria the employee is being measured against. Finally, the system must be appropriate for the job the employee is in.

TYPES OF APPRAISAL SYSTEMS. Performance appraisal systems have two components: one part is the criteria against which the employee is measured (for example, quality of work, knowledge, attitude); the other is the rating scale showing what the employee can achieve or perform on each criteria (good, 5 out of 10, 100 percent, etc). There are two basic types of appraisal systems—subjective and objective.

A *subjective performance* appraisal system is so called because of the subjective (personal) viewpoint from which the appraiser makes his or her observations. Because of lack of specific criteria (described factors of performance) and of specific rating scales (increasing or decreasing descriptors of performance), the subjective appraisal system can result in the citing of critical incidents, comparisons to other employees, and judgments based on personality traits (positive and negative).

With the *objective performance* appraisal system both the criteria for evaluation and the method of measurement are specific. The employee knows what criteria the performance appraisal will be based on and what the measures will be (how does performance measure up to the goals). In this system the employee and the manager establish goals together. They know what performance is based on and how it will be measured. Feedback is provided through reports. The employee knows where he or she stands at all times. This system is a derivation of management by objectives (MBO) and appraisal by results.

METHODS OF APPRAISAL. There are four methods of performance appraisal. These methods are:

- Manager appraisal of subordinate.
- Subordinate self-appraisal.
- Peer appraisal (employees evaluate their peers).
- Upward appraisal (the subordinate evaluates the superior, using a subjective system).

IMPLEMENTING PERSONNEL DECISIONS

Through the process of performance appraisal, management acquires information to make employment decisions. In addition to providing information for decisions on pay increases, appraisal provides information for decisions on promotions, transfers, demotions, and separations.

PROMOTIONS. A promotion is a movement by a person into a position of higher pay and greater responsibilities. Promotions reward competence and ambition.

TRANSFERS. A transfer represents a lateral move from one position to another that has similar pay and responsibility levels. Management uses transfers most often to fill temporary vacancies.

DEMOTIONS. A demotion is a movement from one position to another that has less pay or responsibility attached to it. Demotions can be used for punishment, but most organizations refuse it as an option, preferring instead to suspend the employee or assess a financial penalty through the forfeiture of pay.

SEPARATIONS. Separation is the loss of an employee to an organization. Separations can be involuntary (termination by management) or voluntary (retirement or resignation by employee). A temporary separation is called a layoff.

ESSENTIAL TERMS

Match the following essential terms with the proper definitions. The correct answers are located in the key at the end of the chapter.

A. adverse impact
B. demotion
C. development
D. induction
E. management by objectives
F. objective performance appraisal
G. orientation
H. performance appraisal
I. promotion
J. recruitment
K. selection
L. separation
M. staffing
N. subjective performance appraisal
O. training
P. transfer

____ 1. A lateral move from one position to another having similar pay and a similar responsibility level.

____ 2. A formal structured system designed to measure an employee's actual performance against designated performance standards.

____ 3. Preparing an employee for a future, but fairly well-defined job at a higher level.

____ 4. Finding people to meet the organization's demands for special skills, aptitudes, knowledge, and experience.

____ 5. Bringing a person into the work environment, with emphasis on socialization, the work, and the work environment.

_____ 6. The management activity that attempts to attract good people to an organization and to hold on to them.

_____ 7. Movement from one position to another that has less pay or responsibility attached to it.

_____ 8. Appraisal system in which the criteria for performance and the rating scale are defined.

_____ 9. Evaluating applicants and choosing the person who most closely meets job demands.

_____ 10. Imparts skills, knowledge, and attitudes needed by individuals or groups to improve their abilities to perform in their present jobs.

_____ 11. The effect a selection device has when it excludes a significantly greater number of minority group members or women than other groups.

_____ 12. A temporary or permanent way of losing employees.

_____ 13. An approach to appraisal that requires subordinates to negotiate goals along with priorities and timetables with their supervisors.

_____ 14. Providing a person entering a company with the necessary information about the company.

_____ 15. Appraisal system in which the criteria for performance and the rating scale are not specifically defined.

_____ 16. Movement of a person into a position of higher pay and greater responsibilities.

BRAIN TEASERS

Write the answers to the following "brain teasers."

1. Explain the staffing process. List and explain each step in the staffing process.

2. Distinguish between the goals of equal employment opportunity legislation and affirmative action legislation.

3. Discuss human resource planning. Include in your answer the three components and an explanation of each.

4. Discuss recruitment. Include in your answer a definition and an explanation of the sources.

5. Discuss selection. Include in your answer a definition, the steps in the selection process, and an explanation of each step in the process.

6. Distinguish between induction and orientation.

7. Distinguish between training and development.

8. Discuss performance appraisal. Include in your answer the purposes of performance appraisal and a discussion of objective and subjective systems.

RAPID REVIEW

Complete the following sentences with the appropriate words. The correct answers are located in the key at the end of the chapter.

1. ________________ is a movement by a person into a position of higher pay and greater responsibilities.
2. Three types of tests that may be administered during the selection process are ________________, ________________, and ________________.
3. ________ ________ legislation is designed to eliminate the present effects of past discrimination.
4. A ________________ is a lateral move from one position to another while a ________________ is a move to a position with less pay or responsibility.
5. An ________________ appraisal system has defined criteria for performance and a defined rating scale.

STUDENT EXERCISE

This exercise is designed for you to investigate the staffing function.

STEP 1. Visit a personnel office of a large or medium-sized company in your community. During your visit try to obtain answers to the following questions.

- What steps do your managers go through to have a *new* position approved?
- Do you have job descriptions and job specifications for all jobs? Why or why not?

- What are the sources from which you recruit?
- What methods do you use to recruit candidates?
- Describe the normal selection process.

STEP 2. Summarize your findings in relationship to the chapter material.

ANSWER KEY

ESSENTIAL TERMS

1. P	5. G	9. K	13. E
2. H	6. M	10. O	14. D
3. C	7. B	11. A	15. N
4. J	8. F	12. L	16. I

RAPID REVIEW

1. promotion
2. aptitude, performance, personality
3. affirmative action
4. transfer, demotion
5. objective

CHAPTER

10 Human Motivation

LEARNING OBJECTIVES

After reading and discussing this chapter, you should be able to:

1. Define this chapter's essential terms.
2. Discuss the factors that stimulate and influence motivation.
3. List and give an example of the five need levels.
4. Discuss the impact of hygiene and motivation factors in the work environment.
5. Explain the characteristics of a person with high achievement needs.
6. Discuss the relationship of a person's expectations to motivated behavior.
7. Explain the relationship of reinforcement to motivation.
8. Explain how a person's level of motivation is influenced by equity.

OVERVIEW

MOTIVATION DEFINED

Motivated workers are often described as those who appear willing to exert more effort, to try harder, to accomplish their goals. The question becomes—"What caused the worker to behave in this way?"

THE MOTIVATION MODEL. The needs of a person provide the basis for a motivation model. Needs are deficiencies a person is experiencing at a particular time. The needs may be physiological or psychological. The needs create a tension (stimulus) that results in wants. The person then develops a behavior or set of behaviors to satisfy the wants.

THE INTEGRATED MOTIVATION MODEL. We have identified the foundation for motivation. But there are influences on the behavior of a person that require a more integrative approach.

Once again, unsatisfied needs stimulate wants. As the person is choosing a behavior to satisfy the need, he or she must evaluate past experiences (with the situation at hand), environmental influences (values and expectations of the organization), and perceptions (effort to achieve performance, value of the reward, value in relation to what peers have received for the same effort). In addition to these three variables, skills (the person's capabilities for performing) and incentives (positive and negative factors developed by management to encourage workers to perform a task) are also being evaluated by the person. This leads us to our definition of motivation—the interaction of a person's internalized needs and external influences, which determines behavior designed to achieve a goal.

MOTIVATION THEORIES THAT FOCUS ON NEEDS

Motivation theories provide a manager with insight into motivated behavior. There are three theories that focus on employee needs: Maslow's hierarchy of needs theory, Herzberg's two-factor theory, and McClelland's need-achievement theory.

MASLOW'S HIERARCHY OF NEEDS. Maslow's hierarchy of needs is based on four premises:

1. Only an unsatisfied need can influence behavior.
2. A person's needs are arranged in priority order.
3. As the person's needs are met on one level, the person advances up to the next level of needs.
4. If satisfaction is not maintained for a once-satisfied need, it will become a priority again.

The hierarchy has five need levels:

- Physiological (physical) needs. These are the primary needs: water, air, food, shelter, and avoidance of pain.
- Safety needs. This level describes our need to be free from assault, tyranny, and other threats to our physical and emotional sense of security.
- Love (affiliation or social) needs. These needs describe the desire for friendship, companionship, and a place in the crowd.
- Esteem needs. This category includes the desire for self-respect and for the recognition of one's abilities by others.
- Self-actualization (self-realization) needs. This level of needs refers to the desire for fulfillment.

As a manager works with this theory he or she must remember:

- The theory is a general needs theory.
- People can seek different ways to satisfy one need.
- A thwarted need can cause frustration for an employee and will be a force on an employee until it is satisfied.
- The level of satisfaction of needs always fluctuates.

HERZBERG'S TWO-FACTOR THEORY. The two-factor theory describes one set of factors (motivators) that produce job satisfaction and motivation and another set of factors (hygiene) that leads to job dissatisfaction.

The hygiene factors are part of a job's environment—its context, not its content. When an employer fails to provide these factors in sufficient quality and quantity, job dissatisfaction results. When they are provided in sufficient quality and quantity they will not necessarily act as motivators—they will only lead employees to experience no job dissatisfaction. These factors include:

- salary
- job security
- working conditions
- status
- company policies
- quality of technical supervision
- quality of interpersonal relations among peers, supervisors, and subordinates

The motivation factors are the primary cause of job satisfaction. They relate directly to the real nature (job content) of the work people perform. When an employer fails to provide these factors in sufficient quality, employees will experience no job satisfaction. When they are provided in sufficient quality, they affect and provide job satisfaction and high performance. These factors include:

- achievement
- recognition
- responsibility
- advancement
- work itself
- possibility of growth

Managers who work with this theory must remember:

- This theory relates specifically to the work environment, while Maslow's is a general theory applying to all environments.
- Management can use this theory to focus its effort on ensuring the presence and quality of the hygiene and motivation factors as a foundation on which to build motivation.

McCLELLAND'S NEED-ACHIEVEMENT THEORY. A third needs theory relates to three needs:

- Achievement—desire to excel or achieve in relation to a set of standards.
- Power—desire to control others or have influence over others.
- Affiliation—desire for friendship, cooperation, and close interpersonal relationships.

Most of the study on the subject has focused on achievement motivation. There are two points of note. It was observed that a strong achievement need was related to how well individuals were motivated to perform their work tasks. In addition, it was discovered that the achievement need could be strengthened by training. The person who is described as a high achiever has the following characteristics:

- Achievers have a compelling need for personal achievement in doing the job or task, rather than for the rewards associated with the job.
- Achievers prefer to take personal responsibility for solving their problems rather than leaving the outcome to others.
- Achievers prefer to set moderate goals they think they can achieve.
- Achievers prefer immediate and concrete feedback on performance.

Managers who work with this theory must remember:

- To identify and to work with individuals with high achievement motivation.
- To provide immediate feedback to achievers.

MOTIVATION THEORIES THAT FOCUS ON BEHAVIORS

There are three theories indicating why people choose a particular behavior to satisfy their needs: expectancy theory, reinforcement theory, and equity theory.

EXPECTANCY THEORY. Vroom's expectancy theory states that individuals will evaluate various behavior strategies on these bases: (1) the effort required for performance, (2) whether the performance will have a desired outcome, and (3) how valuable that outcome is to an employee. It includes three variables:

- Valence. (How attractive is the reward?) This is the strength or importance of the reward to the individual.
- Instrumentality. (What is the possibility of a certain performance leading to a desired reward or outcome?) This deals with the potential to achieve the desired outcome as the result of performance.
- Expectation. (Will the effort achieve performance?) This entails an evaluation of how much effort the performance will take and the probability of the effort achieving performance.

Managers who work with this theory must remember:

- The expectancy theory is heavily influenced by people's perceptions of outcomes to specific kinds of behavior. A manager needs to know each individual well.
- Managers need to find out what outcomes are desirable to employees, effectively communicate desired behaviors, link rewards to performance, set attainable performance levels, and provide guidance and direction.

REINFORCEMENT THEORY. Reinforcement theory emphasizes that the behavior of a person in a situation is influenced by the rewards or penalties that person experiences in a similar situation. The theory introduces a major point for managers to understand about motivation—that much of motivated behavior is learned behavior.

There are three main types of reinforcement behaviors available to managers:

- Positive reinforcement (reward) is provided after the desired behavior occurs, with the intention of increasing the probability that the desired behavior will be repeated.
- Punishment (negative) is an attempt to decrease the likelihood of a behavior recurring by applying negative consequences.
- Ignoring is an attempt to provide neither negative nor positive reinforcement. The supervisor's hope is that the misbehavior will be dropped in a short time; that it will go away or disappear if ignored.

Managers who work with this theory must remember:

- Motivated behavior is influenced by learning what is acceptable and not acceptable to the organization.
- Managers need to tell individuals what they are doing wrong, be careful not to reward all individuals the same, tell individuals what they can do to get positive reinforcement, administer the reinforcement as close to the occurrence as possible, and recognize that failure to reward can also modify behavior.

EQUITY THEORY. This theory is based on the assumption that people are motivated by a desire to be equitably treated at work. People determine equity through the calculation of a simple ratio: what effort they are expected to invest on the job (their input) in relation to what they can expect to receive after investing that effort (their outcome or reward). This input/outcome ratio is then compared to the ratios of other individuals or groups. Equity exists when the ratios are equivalent. Inequity exists when, in the employee's mind, inputs exceed the relative or perceived values of the outcomes.

As a manager works with this theory she or he must remember:

- Managers need to be concerned that an employee's motivation is affected by both the absolute rewards and the relative rewards available in the system.
- Employees do make conscious comparisons of equity that influence their motivation levels.
- There should be conscious efforts to establish and retain equity in the work environment.

MANAGING MOTIVATION

There are two practical applications of theory available to develop motivated workers. Managers can focus on the redesign of the job and on the creation of a supportive climate.

JOB REDESIGN. Jobs and organizations have been reexamined and redesigned in the light of modern motivational theories in order to put the challenge and other psychological rewards into work. The two directions approached in redesigning jobs are job scope and job depth. Job scope refers to the variety of tasks incorporated into the job, whereas job depth refers to the degree of discretion the person has to alter the job. The attempts at job redesign include:

- Job enlargement, which increases the variety or the number of tasks, not the quality or the challenge of those tasks.
- Job rotation, which assigns people to different jobs on a temporary basis. The idea is to add variety and to help people understand the dependence of one job on others.

- Job enrichment. Job enrichment applies motivation factors to a job. It concentrates on variety of tasks, task importance, task responsibility, and feedback.

CREATING A SUPPORTIVE CLIMATE. An essential to the development of motivated employees is for a manager to develop a climate in which needs can be met. In addition to adequate resources for goal accomplishment, support for reward systems, training, and a well-conceived organizational format, a supportive climate is shaped by:

- The manager's personal philosophy. The philosophy a manager has about work, people, his or her role in the organization, discipline, coaching, training, or other interpersonal roles form a basis for any action a manager implements.
- The manager's actions. Actions that build a supportive climate include assisting in the attainment of his or her goals, appreciating the contributions of the employee, and being sensitive to the employee's need for equity.
- The manager's expectations. Management expectations need to be developed and communicated to employees. There are two phases to the process. The first consists in developing and communicating the expectations. The second involves consistency: the manager must be consistent in these expectations and in communicating them.

ESSENTIAL TERMS

Match the following essential terms with the proper definitions. The correct answers are located in the key at the end of the chapter.

A. equity theory
B. expectancy theory
C. hygiene factors
D. job enlargement
E. job enrichment
F. job rotation
G. motivation
H. motivation factors
I. needs
J. reinforcement theory

_____ 1. Increases in the variety or number of tasks the job includes, not the quality or challenge of those tasks.

_____ 2. Physical or psychological conditions in humans that act as stimuli for behavior until satisfactions for them have been provided or achieved.

_____ 3. Herzberg's list of causes most closely identified

with unhappiness on the job.

_____ 4. A motivation theory that states that people are influenced in their behavior choices through the comparison of relative input/outcome ratios.

_____ 5. Sending people to different jobs on a rotating or temporary basis.

_____ 6. A motivation theory stating that the behavior choices of a person are influenced by the supervisor's reactions to them and the rewards or penalties experienced in a similar situation.

_____ 7. Herzberg's list of conditions that can lead to an individual's job satisfaction.

_____ 8. A motivation theory stating that a person's behavior is influenced by the value of the rewards, the relationship of the rewards to the performance necessary, and the effort required for performance.

_____ 9. Designing a job to provide more responsibility, control, feedback, and authority for decision-making.

_____ 10. The interaction of a person's internalized needs and external influences (equity, expectancy, and previous conditioning), which determines behavior designed to achieve a goal.

BRAIN TEASERS

Write the answers to the following "brain teasers."

1. Discuss motivation. In your answer, define motivation and the components of the motivation model.

2. Discuss Maslow's hierarchy of needs. In your answer, give the basic assumptions of the model, the five need levels, and the model's implications for a manager.

3. Discuss Herzberg's two-factor theory. In your answer, list each type of factor, explain each, and state the theory's implications for a manager.

4. Discuss McClelland's need-achievement theory. In your answer, explain the three motivation factors and give the theory's implications for a manager.

5. Discuss expectancy theory. Explain the three components of the theory.

6. Discuss reinforcement theory. In your answer, explain the three types of actions available to a manager.

7. Discuss equity theory. In your answer, explain input/outcome ratios and how equity is determined between individuals.

8. Differentiate between job enlargement, job rotation, and job enrichment.

9. Discuss how a manager can create a supportive climate.

RAPID REVIEW

Complete the following sentences with the appropriate words. The correct answers are in the key at the end of the chapter.

1. Maslow's hierarchy of needs includes ________________, ________________, ________________, ________________, and ________________.
2. The three needs noted by McClelland are ________________, ________________, and ________________.
3. Herzberg's list of causes identified with unhappiness on the job are ________________.
4. ________ ________ increases the variety or the number of tasks a job includes, not the quality or challenge of those tasks.
5. Sending people to different jobs on a rotation or temporary basis is known as ________________.

STUDENT EXERCISE

This exercise is designed for you to evaluate the work environment of your company.

STEP 1. Read the following statements describing the work environment of your company.

STEP 2. Rate your environment by placing a number next to each statement using a scale of 1 (low) to 10 (high).

	Statements	Rating
1.	The wages I receive are satisfactory.	( )
2.	The working conditions are satisfactory.	( )
3.	The supervision I receive on the job is satisfactory.	( )
4.	The professional relationship with my superior is satisfactory.	( )
5.	The interpersonal relationship with my superior is satisfactory.	( )
6.	The work I do provides me with satisfaction.	( )
7.	The work I do provides recognition.	( )
8.	The work I do provides opportunities for growth.	( )
9.	The work I do provides a chance for advancement.	( )
10.	The work I do provides opportunity for additional responsibility.	( )
11.	The work I do provides opportunity for achievement.	( )

STEP 3. Add up your score and compare:

0–40	You've got trouble.
41–65	There's hope.
66–85	That's more like it.
86–110	Is there an opening?

ANSWER KEY

ESSENTIAL TERMS

1. D	3. C	5. F	7. H	9. E
2. I	4. A	6. J	8. B	10. G

RAPID REVIEW

1. physiological, safety, love, esteem, self-actualization
2. achievement, power, affiliation
3. hygiene factors
4. job enlargement
5. job rotation

CHAPTER

11 Leadership

LEARNING OBJECTIVES

After reading and discussing this chapter, you should be able to:

1. Define this chapter's essential terms.
2. Discuss leadership as the result of the interaction of the leader, the led, and the work environment.
3. List and briefly explain the four essential leadership roles managers play.
4. Discuss the three factors that comprise a manager's leadership style.
5. Discuss the concept of situational leadership.
6. Discuss Fiedler's contingency theory.
7. Discuss the path–goal theory of leadership.

OVERVIEW

LEADERSHIP DEFINED

Whenever one person influences an individual or group toward accomplishing an objective, leadership occurs. Leadership is thus defined as the process of influencing a group or individual to set or achieve a goal. It is a process involving the leader, the led (group or individual), and a particular goal or situation.

LEADERSHIP ROLES

As a manager interacts with employees in the work environment there are four basic leadership roles that he or she must play—educator, counselor, judge, and spokesperson.

EDUCATOR. All managers provide leadership through performing the educator role. Managers teach job skills, acceptable behavior, and organizational values through the execution of their daily routines. In addition, managers are ultimately responsible for the formal training of their employees.

COUNSELOR. This role involves listening, giving advice, and preventing and solving employees' problems. In performing this role, managers are fulfilling two expectations of employees: awareness of and concern for the individual employee, and assistance in solving a problem.

JUDGE. Playing the leadership role of judge involves appraising subordinates' performances; enforcing policies, procedures, and regulations; settling disputes; and dispensing justice.

SPOKESPERSON. Managers act as spokespersons for subordinates when they relay their suggestions, concerns, and points of view to higher authorities. In performing this leadership role a manager must be willing to represent a subordinate's view, even when the manager disagrees with it.

THE NATURE OF LEADERSHIP

Leadership is a result of the interaction among the superior (leader), the subordinates (the led), and the organizational environment (work and the work situation). Leadership is in essence a special relationship between each manager and each individual or group, a relationship that in turn is influenced by the work environment.

THE LEADER. The manager affects the leadership situation by his or her managerial philosophy, values, needs, and the strengths of and preferences for his or her leadership style.

- *Managerial philosophy.* A manager's philosophy about work and the people who perform the work will influence his or her approach to leadership. A manager operating from Theory X would be directive. A manager whose philosophy is founded on Theory Y would be willing to work with people as individuals, to involve people in the decision-making process, to openly encourage people to seek responsibility, and to work with people to achieve goals.
- *Managerial values.* The values a manager has will influence the leadership environment. If the manager values independence, individual responsibility, initiative, and personal accountability, these values will be reflected in the managerial expectations, which in turn will shape the work environment.
- *Managerial needs.* The need level a manager is functioning on may influence a manager's style. A high need for safety may result in the manager's being reluctant to let employees make decisions for fear of their mistakes.
- *Managerial leadership strengths and preferences.* Each manager has individual strengths or possibly preferences for an approach in

working with people. This preference or strength will serve as the predominant leadership style, because the manager is more comfortable with it or has had success in its application.

THE LED. Individual employees have values, needs, abilities, and style preferences or expectations of a manager that influence the manager's approach.

- *Values of the work group.* A work group valuing independence, unilateral decision making, quality of work life, and opportunity for initiative can influence a manager to allow involvement and participation.
- *Needs of the individuals.* The needs of the individuals being supervised require a response in the manager's leadership style. An employee who exhibits a high concern for security will require leadership different from an employee who is adventurous and seeks new areas of challenge.
- *Ability levels of employees.* An employee who has just been hired without previous experience will function better with close, directive supervision. The experienced worker would chafe under the same close supervision. Hersey and Blanchard developed the life cycle theory of leadership to explain the changes in leadership necessary to respond to the organizational maturity of employees.
- *Leadership style expectations and preferences of individuals.* Individuals and groups have leadership style expectations and preferences. A manager using an unexpected or unpreferred style can cause confusion and indecision on the part of subordinates.

THE ENVIRONMENT. The variables in the work environment that influence the choice of leadership style are the degree of structuring of the job, the amount of technology in the work environment, and the influence of upper-level management.

- *Structure and technology.* Both a highly structured and a highly automated work environment indicate that a directive leadership style is called for. Other combinations of the variables require different leadership styles.
- *Influence of upper-level management.* Upper-level management may influence a subordinate manager's leadership style. This can be done through example or expressed preference.

LEADERSHIP STYLES

The approaches a manager uses to influence others are elements of the manager's leadership style. A manager's leadership style is composed of three parts: how the manager chooses to motivate, her or his decision-making style, and her or his areas of emphasis (orientation) in the work environment.

POSITIVE OR NEGATIVE MOTIVATION. Leaders influence others toward goal achievement through their approach to motivation. Positive leadership style deals in praise and recognition, monetary rewards, increase in security, and the addition of responsibility. Negative leadership emphasizes penalties, loss of job, suspension, and public reprimands.

DECISION-MAKING STYLE. A second element of a manager's leadership style concerns the degree of decision-making authority the manager grants to subordinates. These styles may range from absolute decision making by the manager, with no opportunity for participation by the subordinates, to decision making by the group within limits defined by the manager. The leadership styles developed on a continuum of leadership behavior are grouped under three headings: autocratic, participative, and free-rein.

- *The autocratic leadership style.* This style describes decision making solely by the manager. In its extreme case the manager makes the decision and announces it to the group. Variations of this approach find the manager making the decision and then "selling" it to employees, or making the decision and allowing the group the opportunity to ask questions.
- *The participative leadership approach.* This style is characterized by the manager's involving the subordinates in the decision. The involvement may range from the manager's:

    1. presenting a tentative solution subject to change based on employee input, to
    2. presenting a problem to the employees, soliciting their input, and making the decision, to
    3. defining the limits of the problem and letting the employees make the decision, to
    4. making the decision jointly with the employees.

- *The free-rein style of leadership.* This style is characterized by the leader's encouraging the individual or group to function independently. The leader either sets limits and the followers work out their own problems, or the individuals set their own goals. In this style, the leader's role is to serve as a logistics specialist or representative of the group to outside groups.

TASK ORIENTATION AND EMPLOYEE ORIENTATION. The final element of leadership is the manager's perspective on the most effective way to get work done. The key areas are task orientation and employee orientation.

- *Managerial task orientation.* A manager who favors task orientation places emphasis on getting the work done through better methods or equipment, control of the work environment, assigning and organizing work, one-person decision making, and monitoring through evaluation of performance.
- *Managerial employee orientation.* An employee orientation emphasizes concern for the human needs of subordinates. The approach is to view employees as valuable assets to be cultivated and developed. Teamwork, positive relationships, trust, and solutions of employees' problems are the major focus of the employee-oriented manager.

In actuality, these two perspectives are not mutually exclusive. A manager normally has some degree of both factors. The managerial grid, developed by Blake and Mouton, illustrates the combination of the two perspectives.

LEADERSHIP IS SITUATIONAL. The manager adjusts the decision-making approach and motivational approach in terms of the situation. In addition, the perspective a manager has on the way to get results (emphasis on people or task or both) will affect the chosen style. The choices a manager makes will depend on the situation—individual employees, groups of employees, type of work, structure, personal preference of the manager, and upper-level management's influence.

LEADERSHIP THEORIES

There have been two theories of leadership developed incorporating these situational elements: Fiedler's contingency theory and House's path–goal theory.

FIEDLER'S CONTINGENCY THEORY. Fred E. Fiedler holds that the most appropriate style of leadership for a manager depends on the situation in which a manager works. The contingency model shows that the effectiveness of a leader is determined by the interaction of the manager's orientation (task or employee) with three situational variables:

- *Leader-member relations.* This variable refers to the degree to which the leader is or feels accepted by the group. It is measured by the degree of respect, confidence, and trust subordinates feel toward the superior.
- *Task structure.* This variable concerns the nature of the subordinate's job or task. It reflects the degree of structure in the job: a structured job would be routine in nature with prescribed processes. An unstructured job would have complexity and variety and room for productivity.
- *Leader position power.* This variable describes the organizational

power base from which the individual manager operates. The power can range from strong to weak.

The interaction of the three variables in combination describes the appropriate orientation style for a manager to assume. Task-oriented leaders perform best with either low or high concentrations of power and influence. Employee-oriented leaders perform best with moderate power, control, and influence over the situation.

PATH–GOAL THEORY. The path–goal theory of leadership is concerned with the ways in which a leader can influence a subordinate's motivation, goals, and attempts at achievement. It suggests that a leadership style is effective or ineffective on the basis of how the leader influences the perceptions of (1) work goals or rewards of subordinates and (2) paths that lead to successful accomplishment.

Founded on the expectancy theory of motivation, the path–goal theory states that the leader can influence the perceptions of rewards associated with goals and can clarify what employees have to do to achieve the rewards. The components of the theory are leader behavior and situational factors.

- *Leader behavior.* Leader behavior influences both the goal attractiveness and the paths available to reach the goals. There are four types of leadership behaviors, based on the work needed: instrumental behavior, supportive behavior, participative behavior, and achievement-oriented behavior. These leadership behaviors are based on the situational factors.
- *Situational factors.* There are two situational factors that can influence leadership behavior: (1) the personal characteristics of the subordinates, and (2) the environmental pressures and demands with which subordinates must cope to accomplish goals and satisfy personal needs.

These situational factors do influence a manager's behavior. An employee who has high confidence and ability can be approached with an achievement-oriented style, while a worker who is unsure but has ability can be approached in a supportive manner.

ESSENTIAL TERMS

Match the following essential terms with the proper definition. The correct answers are located in the key at the end of the chapter.

A. contingency model ____ 1. A leadership theory

B. continuum of leadership behavior
C. leadership
D. life cycle theory
E. managerial grid
F. path–goal theory

concerned with the ways in which a leader can influence a subordinate's motivation, goals, and attempts at goal achievement.

____ 2. Tannenbaum and Schmidt's visual representation of various leadership approaches.

____ 3. Blake and Mouton's visual representation of possible leadership behaviors, of which the one that occurs will result from the leader's orientation.

____ 4. A theory of leadership (Fiedler's) that holds that effectiveness of a leader is determined by the interaction of the leader's behavior and three variables: leader–member relations, task structure, leader position power.

____ 5. The process of influencing the group or individual toward the accomplishment of goal setting or goal achievement.

____ 6. A theory of leadership that states that the leadership approach varies with the maturity of the individual.

BRAIN TEASERS

Write the answers to the following "brain teasers."

1. Discuss leadership. In your discussion, define leadership and explain the four leadership roles.

2. Discuss situational leadership. In your answer, explain the interaction of the three leadership variables.

3. Discuss leadership styles. In your answer, explain each element of a manager's leadership style (motivation, decision making, and orientation).

4. Discuss Fiedler's contingency theory. In your answer, explain the four variables that interact to determine leadership styles.

5. Discuss the path–goal theory. In your answer, discuss the leadership and situational variables.

RAPID REVIEW

Complete the following sentences with the appropriate words. The correct answers are in the key at the end of the chapter.

1. A decision-making leadership style in which employees are involved in the decision is called ________________.

2. A manager who focuses on better methods to achieve results has a ________________ -oriented style of leadership.
3. A leadership role that requires the manager to evaluate performance is the ________________ role.
4. According to Fiedler, the three variables that interact with the orientation of a manager are ________________, ________________, and ________________.
5. The leadership situation is a result of the interaction of the ________________, the ________________, and the ________________.

STUDENT EXERCISE

This exercise is designed to assist you in investigating leadership styles.

STEP 1. Interview a manager of a public utility or local government in your community, seeking answers to the following questions:

- What decisions do you make personally?
- How do you involve your subordinates in decision-making?
- What decisions are made by your subordinates?
- Do you consider yourself an autocratic, participative, or free-rein leader? Give examples.
- Do you find it necessary to adjust your leadership style? Why?

STEP 2. Interview a manager of a rapidly growing business in your community and obtain answers to the questions in Step 1.

STEP 3. Summarize the results of your interviews and compare the differences and similarities of the information from each interview.

ANSWER KEY

ESSENTIAL TERMS

1. F	3. E	5. C
2. B	4. A	6. D

RAPID REVIEW

1. participative
2. task
3. judge
4. leader–member relations, task structure, leader position power
5. leader, led, environment

CHAPTER

12 Controlling: Prevention and Coping

LEARNING OBJECTIVES

After reading and discussing this chapter, you should be able to:

1. Define this chapter's essential terms.
2. Explain the interrelationship of planning and controlling.
3. Discuss the three steps in the control process.
4. Explain the concept of managerial standards.
5. Explain the concept of technical standards.
6. Discuss prevention, feedforward, and feedback controls.
7. List and discuss the six characteristics a manager must consider in designing a control system.
8. Explain two factors for making controls effective.

OVERVIEW

THE NEED FOR CONTROLS

Controlling is the last function of management. It is last because it is the function that monitors all other functions. Only through controlling can efficiency and effectiveness be maintained.

CONTROLLING DEFINED

Control has been defined as determining whether people and the various parts of the organization are on target, achieving their plans. While control interacts with all functions of management, it is most closely allied with planning. This is because plans form the foundation for controlling.

THE CONTROL PROCESS

Controlling consists of a three-step process: establishing standards, measuring performance, and taking corrective action.

ESTABLISHING STANDARDS. The establishment of standards means that the manager knows what is expected. This information is available from good plans. Standards focus on the goals and objectives of the organization.

MEASURING PERFORMANCE. If standards exist and performance is measured, it is then possible to note where differences exist. Performance can be greater than, equal to, or below standards. If performance does not match standards, then the next step is in order.

TAKING CORRECTIVE ACTION. Any difference between standards and performance is considered a deviation. When a deviation exists, either the plan (standards) or performance must be corrected.

TYPES OF CONTROLS

Control systems generally are developed to provide one of three categories of information. These three categories, prevention, feedforward, and feedback controls, are differentiated by the time frame in which information and action are placed.

PREVENTION CONTROLS. Prevention controls establish conditions that will make it difficult or impossible for deviations from the norm to occur. This type of control is in place before actions begin and blocks activities that are not desired.

FEEDFORWARD CONTROLS. Feedforward controls are future-directed, in that they are designed to detect and anticipate deviations from standards at various points when a system is operational. There are two types of feed-forward controls: diagnostic and therapeutic. Diagnostic controls include such items as meters, warning lights and alarms, and other devices that indicate that something is not right. Therapeutic controls not only detect deviations but take corrective action.

FEEDBACK CONTROLS. Feedback controls are postaction controls and focus on the end results of the process. A feedback control provides information for a manager to examine and apply to future activities that are similar to the present one. The purpose is to help prevent mistakes in the future.

CONTROL CHARACTERISTICS

Many factors must be taken into consideration when designing a control system. The following questions pinpoint some of the major issues.

1. Does the organization understand the purpose and intended use of the control system?
2. Is the system accepted rather than opposed by members of the organization?
3. Is the system focused on important items that the manager should monitor, or is it based on trivial items?

4. Is the control system accurate? Does it give members of the organization information upon which they can reasonably expect to act?
5. Is the control information generated in a time frame that is quick enough for managers to take corrective actions?
6. Is the control system economically feasible? In other words, does the system pay for itself?

MAKING CONTROLS EFFECTIVE

Controls are effective if they do what they were designed to do and do not create organizational problems. Since controls must be evaluated in terms of what they monitor, it is important that the controls themselves be continuously monitored. This ensures that a control system is telling the manager what he or she needs and that the system is not out-of-date. Employees should be involved in the design of control systems. The employees who will ultimately implement the system will be more accepting of and committed to the system if they are involved early. Also, controls must be realistic. They must not over-control or be arbitrary.

Controls should be adapted to the organization, not the organization to the controls. Keeping these things in mind will enable the manager to be sensitive to the impact controls have on organizations. They will also make control systems more effective.

ESSENTIAL TERMS

Match the following essential terms with the proper definition. The correct answers are located in the key at the end of the chapter.

A. controlling
B. diagnostic control
C. feedback control
D. feedforward control
E. prevention control
F. standard
G. therapeutic control

____ 1. A monitoring device or system designed to sense what deviations from standards are taking place and why, and then to take a corrective action.

____ 2. A quantitative or qualitative measuring device designed to help monitor the performances of people, capital goods, or processes.

____ 3. A monitoring system or device designed to detect and to anticipate deviations from standards at various points throughout an ongoing process.

____ 4. A monitoring device or system that attempts to determine what deviation from a standard is taking or has taken place.

____ 5. Establishing performance standards used to measure progress toward a goal.

____ 6. A monitoring device or system designed to provide end-result information on a project for future planning.

____ 7. A monitoring device or system designed to establish conditions that will make it difficult or impossible for deviations to occur.

BRAIN TEASERS

Write the answers to the following "brain teasers."

1. Why is it said that controlling is nothing more than planning seen from a different view?

2. How do the three steps of controlling tie in with the planning process? Specifically, which step(s) in planning and control overlap?

3. What are the differences between managerial and technical standards?

4. Of the six characteristics a manager must consider in designing a control system, which two do you feel to be the most critical? Why?

5. What is the major value of each of the following categories of control: Prevention? Feedforward? Feedback?

6. Why must a manager be concerned with the effectiveness of controls? What criteria would you use to measure such effectiveness?

RAPID REVIEW

Complete the following by marking each statement true or false. The correct answers are located in the key at the end of the chapter.

_______ 1. A salesperson who has a quota of $15,000 per month in sales and averages $20,000 per month is not of concern to a control system because of her continuing success.

_______ 2. Corrective action may be automatic, not requiring human intervention.

_______ 3. Job descriptions and job specifications are examples of feedback controls.

_______ 4. Controls, because of their complexity, should be designed only by highly trained managerial specialists.

_______ 5. Part of the purpose of management control is to undertake a systematic effort to set performance standards in line with planning objectives.

STUDENT EXERCISE

The purpose of this exercise is to assist you in understanding the general purpose and uses of control systems. When you have finished, you should be able to define at least one type of control system and its use.

STEP 1. Read a journal article on control as it is used in a business.

STEP 2. After reading the article, write your thoughts about the control system asking yourself the following questions:

- Is it effective?
- Would it work in a business you might wish to open?
- Would it provide you with information not previously considered that would be of use in your business?
- Can you think of a better control mechanism to meet your needs?

ANSWER KEY

ESSENTIAL TERMS

1. G	3. D	5. A	7. E
2. F	4. B	6. C	

RAPID REVIEW

1. False
2. True
3. False
4. False
5. True

CHAPTER

13 Controls

LEARNING OBJECTIVES

After reading and discussing this chapter, you should be able to:

1. Define this chapter's essential terms.
2. Describe the purposes for each of the general management controls.
3. Describe the purposes for each of the financial controls.
4. Describe the purposes for each of the production controls.

OVERVIEW

WHAT FORMS DO CONTROLS TAKE?

There are three broad categories of controls: general management, financial, and production. Each contains several tools and techniques that enable the manager to focus attention on the three specialized areas.

GENERAL MANAGEMENT CONTROLS

The manager must make decisions involving human and non-human resources. To provide the manager with information needed to make those decisions, general management control systems such as *management information systems (MIS), Key Indicator Management (KIM), human asset accounting,* and *inventory control* have been developed. These general management controls can be used in many areas, but each firm will use only those that are effective, efficient, and worth the cost.

MANAGEMENT INFORMATION SYSTEMS (MIS). The purpose of management information systems (MIS) is to collect, sort, interpret, summarize, and distribute vital information to those who need it. In developing an MIS, certain critical factors need to be considered. The MIS must:

1. Meet organizational objectives.
2. Provide information flow.
3. Deliver the right quality and quantity of information.
4. Provide timely information.

An MIS is not totally dependent on a computer, but speed and accuracy are facilitated when a computer is used.

KEY INDICATOR MANAGEMENT. Somewhat different from the MIS, but associated with it, is the Key Indicator Management system (KIM), which provides managers with brief pieces of information that indicate whether or not a deeper look into the remainder of the information is warranted. A well-designed KIM allows the manager to practice "management by exception." Management by exception is the principle that good managers develop guidelines for routine decisions and delegate those decisions to their subordinates. The exceptions to routine decision making are left to managers for resolution.

HUMAN ASSET ACCOUNTING. Human asset accounting is a relatively new concept. It is a system built on the idea that employees represent investments of an organization, not merely expenses (as in traditional accounting). Two new accounting techniques are used. The first compiles a running total of monies spent performing the staffing functions for all personnel. The second computes the dollar contribution each employee makes toward a company's profits.

INVENTORY CONTROL. In any business, inventory represents money that is sitting idle. Merchandise not sold as rapidly as possible costs the firm. However, sales lost due to insufficient inventory also cost. The purpose of inventory control is to optimize the amount of inventory on hand without tying up excessive money. This is accomplished by knowing when and how much to order.

FINANCIAL CONTROLS

Why is financial control so important to a business and a key concern for managers? In profit-oriented businesses, the goal of financial management is profit; in non-profit organizations, the focus is on attaining the maximum level of benefits for clients. Achievement of these two goals represents the maximization of effective and efficient management. There are four common financial control systems: budgets, financial control centers, financial statements, and ratio analysis.

BUDGETS. All organizations use a budget, which is nothing more than a document predicting the amount of money a firm will spend (expenditures) and the amount it will receive (revenue).

The most common budget is the operating budget. This budget examines the costs of providing goods and/or services, including all human and material expenses, and looks at expected revenue. The capital expenditure budget monitors expenditures for adding assets to the firm. The cash budget includes the projections of the amount of cash that will flow into and out of an organization.

FINANCIAL CONTROL CENTERS. Every manager has some responsibility for financial control. This is usually stated as a financial objective for a manager. When responsibility is assigned, the area covered by the assignment is known as a financial control center.

FINANCIAL STATEMENTS. Two major statements exist that afford the manager an opportunity to review and control finances. They are the income statement and the balance sheet. Income statements break down expenditures and revenues into a format that allows the manager to see whether revenues or expenses are in order. The balance sheet is often referred to as the x-ray of the organization. It shows what the firm is worth (assets) and where the money has come from to finance those assets. The two sources of funds used to finance assets are borrowed money (liabilities) and invested owner funds (equity).

RATIO ANALYSIS. Ratio analysis is the use of financial information to determine how well an organization is doing in terms of past performance and current plans, and in relation to other organizations. The financial information is usually analyzed by comparing one item to another. There are three major categories of ratios: liquidity, profitability, and debt ratios.

AUDITS. Audits are checks on the financial practices of an organization. An audit examines the data used to create financial statements and makes a determination as to the data's accuracy. Audits can be made by regular employees or by outside firms that specialize in auditing. The former is called an *internal audit,* while the latter is called an *external audit.*

PRODUCTION CONTROLS

Production control is a technique for ensuring that both schedules and quality production are met. Three principal types of production controls include GANTT charts, network techniques, and quality control.

GANTT CHARTS. The GANTT chart allows the manager to schedule activities and follow up on their execution. The actual scheduling of activities is part of planning. However, once an operation has begun, the manager can check to see if events are proceeding according to schedule in a timely fashion. If activities are not being completed according to schedule, then following events that must be postponed can be identified.

NETWORK TECHNIQUES. Network techniques, such as program evaluation review technique (PERT), are similar to GANTT charts except that they focus on the interrelationship of events and activities. Users of PERT and critical path method (CPM) monitor those events that, in conjunction with each other, require the most time to be completed. This "critical path" is the longest "path" through a project and is another example of a tool that enables the manager to practice management by exception.

QUALITY CONTROL. Quality control ensures that customers receive the highest-quality product. There are many techniques used in quality control. One is inspection, where products are examined in relation to standards designed for them. Another technique is testing, where the product is evaluated in terms of its performance characteristics. Each of the foregoing can be used on all products or on a select few, through sampling. Sampling requires that only a small, randomly selected percentage of a whole population (total number of products) be chosen for inspection or testing. If done correctly, the sample will reflect conditions of all the other products.

COMPUTERS AND CONTROLS

Most control techniques have been converted for computer application. The reason for this is that computers provide speed and accuracy far surpassing that of manually tabulated controls. This allows for timely decisions to be made. To have an effective computer control system, four potential problem areas should be reviewed. They include surveying:

1. Benefits versus costs of the system.
2. The technological environment of the system.
3. The impact of a computer on existing personnel.
4. Centralization versus decentralization of a computer system.

ESSENTIAL TERMS

Match the following essential terms with the proper definition. The correct answers are located in the key at the end of the chapter.

A. audit
B. balance sheet
C. critical path
D. data
E. human asset accounting
F. income statement
G. information
H. Key Indicator Management
I. management information system
J. program evaluation review technique
K. ratio

____ 1. A monitoring and control system using mutually agreed-upon key measures, represented visually and at regular intervals, to judge a manager's or department's progress or lack thereof.

____ 2. A formal method of providing management with accurate and timely information in order for decision-making and managerial functions and operations to be carried out effectively.

_____ 3. The relationship between two or more numbers.

_____ 4. An internal or external method of control, primarily financial, that determines if records, reports, statements, and the data they are based on are correct and in line with established rules and procedures.

_____ 5. The financial statement and control that examines an organization's assets and the ownership interests in them.

_____ 6. The longest sequence of events and activities through a network production schedule.

_____ 7. A network method of production scheduling that assigns more than one time for completion of activities and assigns weights of importance to each time estimate.

_____ 8. The financial statement and control that examines the organization's income and expenses.

_____ 9. A control method that treats the money spent on and for employees as investments rather than expenses.

_____ 10. Data that has been deliberately selected, processed, and organized to be useful to an individual manager.

_____ 11. Facts and figures that have not been processed.

BRAIN TEASERS

Write the answers to the following "brain teasers."

1. What are the major purposes of a MIS, KIM, human asset accounting, and an inventory control system? Which do you believe would be the most reliable general management control system? Why?

2. Of the financial control systems, which is the most exact? Why? Compare it with another and justify your decision.

3. What results would be different if you used a PERT rather than a GANTT chart production control technique?

4. What are the advantages and disadvantages of using computers in a control system?

RAPID REVIEW

Complete the following sentences with the appropriate word. The correct answers are located in the key at the end of the chapter.

1. A ________________ ________________ projects or estimates the amount of cash that will flow in and out of an organization or any of its parts for a fixed period.
2. ________________ ________________ are designed to put the profit picture into perspective.
3. When activities or events are interrelated, ________________ ________________ are good control tools to monitor the completion of events.
4. An ________________ is a method to determine if records, reports, and data are correct and in line with established rules and procedures.
5. An ________________is the financial statement and control that examines the organization's income and expenses.

STUDENT EXERCISE

The completion of this exercise will find you with a better understanding of the potential of production-control techniques.

STEP 1. You are a manufacturer of widgets, a highly sophisticated tool that is used in the defense industry of the United States to monitor foreign activities. There can be no errors in your basic system but there is a tolerance in the gidgets, which make up your widget system: for each of the one hundred gidgets involved in the system, there are ten back-ups.

STEP 2. Using the above information, how would you go about setting up a production-control system to ensure maximum effectiveness and efficiency while cutting costs to your company? Look at both the widgets and the gidgets. An error could result in the elimination of your plant in the event of an enemy attack.

STEP 3. Write up your conclusions, using one more guide: If you expend full inspection efforts, you will not suffer a loss or make a profit.

ANSWER KEY

ESSENTIAL TERMS

1. H	3. K	5. B	7. J	9. E	11. D
2. I	4. A	6. C	8. F	10. G	

RAPID REVIEW

1. cash budget
2. profitability ratios
3. network techniques
4. audit
5. income statement

CHAPTER

14 Maintaining the Organizational Climate: Managing Change and Conflict

LEARNING OBJECTIVES

After reading and discussing this chapter, you should be able to:

1. Define this chapter's essential terms.
2. Explain the concept of organizational climate, and describe its components.
3. Define change, and discuss the sources of change.
4. Identify the phases of change in an organization and the importance of this knowledge to a manager.
5. Explain the Greiner Model for implementing organizational change.
6. Discuss the reasons why people resist change.
7. Discuss two models for changing people's behavior.
8. Explain the purpose of an organizational development program.
9. Identify the potential causes of conflict in an organization.
10. Explain three strategies for conflict management.

OVERVIEW

THE NEED TO UNDERSTAND CHANGE AND CONFLICT

As you already know, an organization consists of two or more people working toward a common goal. However, there are two factors that often disrupt work and/or goal achievement: change and conflict. Change is a shift or alteration in the present environment. Conflict is a disagreement between organizational members resulting from the fact that they must share scarce resources or work activities and/or from the fact that they have different status, goals, values, or perceptions. The manager must recognize and understand the need for change, the seeds of conflict, and kinds of strategies that can help manage both.

THE ORGANIZATIONAL CLIMATE

Change and conflict occur in every organization. They can work for good or bad, depending on how the manager addresses each issue. Without conflict, no change is possible. Without change, no growth is possible.

An organization's ability to sense the need for change, to work through the change process, and to cope successfully with change is determined by its organizational climate. Organizational climate is the organizational personality—its feel or character.

KOTTER MODEL OF ORGANIZATIONAL CLIMATE. Several models have been developed to aid managers in diagnosing organizational climates. One of them, the Kotter model, suggests that all organizations are composed of seven systems—one major or control system and six subsystems. The composite subsystems make up one large system, the organization, which is itself a subsystem of larger systems, such as an industry. The model focuses managerial attention on the fit, or interaction, between each of the organization's subsystems, as well as the activity that is going on within a given subsystem.

The systems within an organization consist of Key Organizational Processes, External Environment, Employee and Other Tangible Assets, Formal Organizational Arrangements, Social Systems, Technology, and the Dominant Coalition. This "open systems" model suggests that the climate of an organization is a compilation of the characterizations of each of the subsystems.

IMPORTANCE OF ORGANIZATIONAL CLIMATE. Climate is the one factor that most influences an organization's ability to change or thwart change. The attitudes of people when fused together create a force that bonds or destroys. Managers must recognize this and work toward creating an organizational climate that is capable of adapting to future needs.

THE NATURE OF CHANGE

Anything that enters into an individual's or organization's perception, organization, or explanation of realty and does not mesh with existing beliefs will cause confusion and conflict. Sometimes individuals and organizations live in confusion and conflict for long periods of time. However, confusion and conflict are motivators for change.

SOURCES OF CHANGE. There are two types of change we encounter. Managed change is when we consciously plan for change. Unplanned-for change is that which surprises the organization but must be dealt with. Additionally, there are many sources of change. External to the organization are such factors as technology, competition, government actions, economic variables, and social values. Within the organization, managerial policies or styles, systems and procedures, and employee attitudes can all be sources of change.

IDENTIFYING THE NEED FOR CHANGE. Larry Greiner has developed a model describing how the maturing organization will inevitably encounter the need for change. The model depicts certain factors that require an organization to make "revolutionary" changes or die. There are five phases, as Greiner sees organizational growth, where change must occur. The first phase emphasizes marketing and gives little attention to management. This is the creative phase. A desire for better management leads to the direction phase, which, once in place, centralizes and produces a desire for autonomy. The direction phase is then replaced by delegation. Once top management feels that it is no longer in control, a fourth phase, coordination, is introduced. Again, paperwork weighs down the organization to the point that a new phase is called for. Collaboration is the final phase, in which flexibility and behaviorally oriented efforts are keys to improved organizational climate.

MANAGING CHANGE

Once a manager recognizes that change is inevitable and desirable, a strategy for managing change is needed.

PHILOSOPHY OF CHANGE. All managers must develop a philosophy toward change. Successful philosophies have included three elements: a concept of trust, organizational learning, and adaptiveness. Trust is an assured reliance on some person or thing, a belief in another. To develop trust, both a sense of individual personal security and a feeling of adequacy must be nurtured. Organizational learning refers to the ability of an organization to recall what it has done in the past and to grow from a reflection on past actions. Adaptiveness is the ability of individuals and organizations to be vulnerable to change and have positive reactions to that vulnerability. All three ingredients must be present for the manager to have an organization that can move from confusion and frustration to change with the minimum of disruptions.

GREINER MODEL FOR ORGANIZATIONAL CHANGE. Greiner has outlined a six-phase process for managing change. Central to the change model is the change agent, the party responsible for making change possible. The model suggests that change occurs when (1) there is pressure and arousal for change and top management is supportive of attempting to make change occur; (2) a change agent then engages in intervention and reorientation, which is setting a mood for change; (3) data is gathered and analyzed in the diagnosis and recognition phase; (4) new strategies for making change possible are explored in the intervention and commitment activity; (5) actual implementation of new ideas is tried as the organization experiments and searches; and (6) acceptable behavior is defined and new ways of interacting established in the last phase, reinforcement and acceptance. Such a model gives a manager a sequence of activities to follow in introducing change to an organization.

RESISTANCE TO CHANGE. Individuals, groups, and organizations resist change for many reasons. Some of these reasons include:

1. Desire for security.
2. Old habits.
3. Selective perceptions.
4. Awareness of weaknesses in the proposed change.

CHANGING PEOPLE'S BEHAVIOR

There are two approaches to changing behavior. Modifying the behavior of an individual or small group is known as staff development, while a change in an entire organization is called organizational development (OD). The following techniques are effective tools for use in staff development.

THE LEWIN MODEL. The Lewin model attempts to neutralize, or unfreeze, behavior-causing problems, and then develop an awareness for a need to change. Once this second phase is accomplished, new behavior is taught and institutionalized, or, in Lewin's terms, refreezing takes place.

FORCE FIELD ANALYSIS. Force field analysis is nothing more than looking at a problem from the perspective of seeing what forces are working for and against an individual in a given situation. After looking at past experiences, negative forces may be overcome by using positive forces that are present. The concept behind this tool is that often we overlook what we have working for us and concentrate only on obstacles. Force field analysis forces the individual to look at positive forces as well as obstacles.

ORGANIZATIONAL DEVELOPMENT

PURPOSES OF OD. The purpose of OD is to bring together a total plan of activities which enables the entire organization to cope with change. In effect, OD primarily exists to assist renewal of the organizational climate.

OD STRATEGIES. A comprehensive strategy to make an entire organization change is called organizational development (OD). There are many approaches to OD, all of which have supporters and detractors. Some of the major ones are training programs, T-groups, team building exercises, Grid OD, MBO programs, job enrichment, and action research.

EVALUATING THE EFFECTIVENESS OF OD. Since OD is an ongoing effort for change, it is important to periodically evaluate OD efforts. The basic tool used is to see if original problems have been overcome or at least accepted. Then, if change has occurred, OD efforts are considered to have been effective.

CONFLICT—ITS NATURE AND SOURCES

Conflict arises because individuals and groups have different resources, values, goals, status, and perceptions. It is inevitable. Conflict can be positive or negative, depending on the manager's skills in addressing it. In addition to differences in perceptions, goals, values and resources, conflict can arise from:

1. Disagreement in role requirements.
2. Nature of work activities.
3. Individual approaches.
4. Stage of organizational development.

MANAGING CONFLICT

PHILOSOPHICAL APPROACHES TO CONFLICT. To manage conflict, a manager must have a notion as to what conflict is and why it exists. There are three philosophical approaches:

1. In the traditional view, conflict is unnecessary and harmful to the organization.
2. The behavioral view sees conflict as natural, because people are present in an organization.
3. The interactionist view sees conflict as not only inevitable but healthy, since it is the basis for change and growth.

STRATEGIES FOR MANAGING CONFLICT. In order for the manager to deal with conflict, he or she must determine:

1. The type of conflict.
2. The source of conflict.
3. The level of conflict.

After that point, a strategy must be developed. There are many kinds. Each has a different objective. One simply desires to reduce the level of conflict. Another attempts to resolve conflict. In resolving conflict, a manager can:

1. Initiate compromise.
2. Initiate integrative problem-solving.
3. Initiate superordinate goals.

A last strategy is to increase the level of conflict. Techniques available include:

1. Bringing in outsiders.
2. Changing the rules.
3. Changing the organization.
4. Changing managers.
5. Encouraging competition.

In any event, conflict will appear and reappear. The successful manager will recognize this and develop strategies to cope with conflict based on the organization's needs at the time conflict emerges.

ESSENTIAL TERMS

Match the following essential terms with the proper definition. The correct answers are located in the key at the end of the chapter.

A. change
B. change agent
C. conflict
D. organizational climate
E. organizational development
F. organizational learning

____ 1. Disagreement between two or more organizational members or groups arising because they must share scarce resources or work activities and/or because they have different status, goals, values, or perceptions.

____ 2. The psychological environment or personality of an organization in which people work.

____ 3. A shift or alteration in the present organizational environment.

____ 4. The long-range program for systematic renewal of an organization that is based on an analysis of organizational problems.

____ 5. The individual responsible for introducing planned change in an organization. He or she may be an insider or an outsider.

_____ 6. The "how" behind the attempts by organizations and their managers to integrate new ideas into established systems to produce better ways of changing things.

BRAIN TEASERS

Write the answers to the following "brain teasers."

1. Realistically, what can a manager do to develop and maintain an organizational climate that will keep the organization adaptive to change?

2. What is the major difference between single-loop and double-loop learning? What are the implications of these concepts to an organization's learning ability?

3. Two models by Larry Greiner are presented in this chapter. One describes when change will occur and the other suggests ways to manage change in an organization. Do you agree or disagree with his models? Why? Can you make any improvements to them?

4. How do conflict, change, and human resistance to change interact? Are there any contradictions in the relationship between these concepts?

5. Can you think of an OD strategy that might be applicable for the place you work? If so, describe the situation and define how your strategy would improve things.

RAPID REVIEW

Complete the following sentences with the appropriate words. The correct answers are in the key at the end of the chapter.

1. The Lewin model for changing behavior consists of three phases: ________________, ________________, and ________________.
2. The ____________ ____________ is that group of managers that makes an organization "click," according to the Kotter model.
3. The three elements that should be included in one's philosophy of change are ____________, ____________ ____________, and ____________.
4. Before any organizational change can occur, top management must be ____________ to the program.
5. Grid OD, MBO, and Team Building are all forms of ____________ ____________.

STUDENT EXERCISE

The purpose of this exercise is to cause you to reflect on problem-solving as a means to bring about change when it appears to be very difficult.

STEP 1. Think of a success you recently enjoyed that required some effort on your part. Also identify a major problem currently facing you that seems to be insurmountable.

STEP 2. On one page, list all of the things that worked for you in achieving your success. Then list those things that almost caused you to fail or created some difficulty in achieving your success. How did you overcome those obstacles?

STEP 3. On a separate page, list those things that are working for you in the problem situation you now face. (There must be some things or you would have already given up!) Next, list the obstacles to your resolving the problem.

STEP 4. Now compare the two lists and look at the forces working for and against you. Are there forces working against you now that also worked against you in the past? If so, how did you overcome them before? Were there strengths present in past situations that you may be overlooking now?

You may wish to review several past successes to recall some forgotten strengths you possess that may be called upon now in order to work toward change.

ANSWER KEY

ESSENTIAL TERMS

1. C	3. A	5. B
2. D	4. E	6. F

RAPID REVIEW

1. unfreezing, change, refreezing
2. dominant coalition
3. trust, organizational learning, adaptiveness
4. committed
5. organizational development

CHAPTER

15 Management and Productivity

LEARNING OBJECTIVES

After reading and discussing this chapter, you should be able to:

1. Define this chapter's essential terms.
2. List three areas in which the federal government has contributed to our nation's decline in productivity and what actions it has taken to improve each area.
3. List two areas in which employees have contributed to our nation's productivity decline and what is being or can be done about each area.
4. List two areas in which organized labor has contributed to our nation's decline in productivity and what is being or can be done about each area.
5. List two areas in which management has contributed to our nation's productivity decline and what is being or can be done about each area.

OVERVIEW

PRODUCTIVITY AS THE KEY TO SUCCESS

The basic measure of the efficiency of business is productivity. Effective businesses concentrate on producing the right product or service for their situation and capabilities. Efficient businesses concentrate on lowering costs or increasing output for each dollar invested in the business.

PRODUCTIVITY DEFINED

Productivity, in its most common form of measurement, is the measurement of how much input is needed to produce an amount of output. Productivity is usually expressed as a ratio between these two items. A productivity index is the result of dividing input into output.

PRODUCTIVITY INDEXES. Two kinds of indexes can be used to measure productivity: the single-factor index and the combined-factors index.

The single factor index might use one of the following as a unit of input: hours of labor, hours of machine time, tons of materials, or dollars invested in capital. A combined-factors index may combine such factors as labor, materials, and capital under some kind of formula and use it as an overall measure of an organization's total productivity gain or loss.

Productivity indexes should be developed for a specific unit. A company would use its own factors while a country might use a ratio of national output of goods and services—gross national product—to the total hours of human labor needed to produce the output. The productivity figures for the United States using this ratio have shown a decline in the rate of U.S. productivity, that is, productivity has been increasing at a decreasing rate. A number of factors have been identified that affect the U.S. rate of productivity. Among them are actions by the government, individual employees, unions, and management.

GOVERNMENT ACTIONS AFFECTING PRODUCTIVITY

The government is a key ingredient in the productivity picture. Through decisions regarding spending and taxation, regulation, and capital investment, the government has affected productivity.

GOVERNMENT AND SPENDING. As the federal budget goes into a deficit position, the government can continue to operate only by borrowing from the public. This places the government in direct competition with business in its efforts to get short- and long-term funding. According to the laws of supply and demand, when the supply of money is limited, the price of money will increase. Thus increased government deficits have raised the cost of borrowing. High interest rates cause businesses and consumers to put off spending. Less capital equipment is purchased, and less is spent for consumer goods. These decreases mean less expansion of business operations and fewer jobs.

GOVERNMENT AND REGULATIONS. The burden of regulating businesses in the United States is left to the government. Over 90,000 persons are involved in this activity. That, in addition to the taxes paid to support the effort, costs business because of the forms and procedures every business must conform to.

GOVERNMENT AND CAPITAL INVESTMENT. The source of business expansion and growth has been monies invested in new equipment and technology. Tax advantages have historically made this profitable. As the cost of money has gone up, the incentive for new investment has declined. In recent years, the United States has ranked last among major industrial nations in terms of the percentage of GNP placed into new investments. This means that our capital base, the plants and equipment used to produce goods, has become obsolete compared to those of other nations.

To help stimulate spending on capital improvements, the federal government has enacted major tax cuts and tax credits for investments in plants and equipment. As a result, capital spending has increased dramatically.

EMPLOYEE ACTIONS AFFECTING PRODUCTIVITY

Today's workers have been accused of not wanting to work, of being in love with leisure at the expense of commitments, of being sloppy, and of lacking pride in accomplishments. The result of these attitudes has been that the quality of work has decreased and, in turn, productivity has decreased.

WORKER ATTITUDES TOWARD WORK. American workers are working harder and longer but are enjoying jobs less. Individuals report the need for more challenging work, recognition, less stress, and better bosses.

EMPLOYEE THEFT. Employee theft accounts for about 70 percent of retailers' losses to all types of crimes. The impact on a victimized company can be serious enough to force it into bankruptcy. Even small losses due to employee theft reduce the company's profits and productivity.

Theft is not limited to goods. It also includes stealing trade secrets and time. Companies can manage these instances of theft by improving training, providing rewards for information, implementing high-technology lenses, and by closer supervision.

DRUGS AT WORK. Another contributing factor to the productivity problem is the illegal use of drugs. It has been estimated that drug use by employees costs their employers billions of dollars each year in lost productivity.

ATTEMPTS TO CAPTURE GREATER COMMITMENT. In order to create an environment in which employees make a greater commitment to an organization, managers must rekindle employee enthusiasm and interest in work. There are many approaches being used. The most common are Quality of Work Life (QWL) and quality circle programs. QWL efforts are intended to aid employees in their search for satisfaction of their needs. Quality circles involve the employee in ways whereby they take more responsibility for work planning and outcomes.

UNION ACTIONS AFFECTING PRODUCTIVITY

RIGID JOB STRUCTURE. Through a combination of union philosophy and management science techniques, management designed a rigid job structure system. Duties and tasks were clearly spelled out. This resulted in the inability of a company to change jobs in the face of a changing market. This, in turn, makes a company, an industry, and a nation less productive.

DEVELOPING PROGRESSIVE LABOR RELATIONS. The traditional approach to American labor-management relations is adversarial. This has led to productivity losses through suspicion and noncooperation. However, there have been some recent actions, through the development of cooperative quality of life programs, that show labor and management can work together.

MANAGEMENT ACTIONS AFFECTING PRODUCTIVITY

POOR MANAGEMENT PRACTICES. The following are ways in which management has contributed to the productivity problem by: sacrificing long-term planning and objectives for short-term gains, frequent executive turnover leading to major changes in strategy, a strategy of corporate diversification, and managers who fail to manage subordinates properly.

COMMITMENT AT THE TOP. Efforts to improve productivity must start at the top of a company. The American Productivity Center has suggested that management follow some basic guidelines to improve management practices. They are:

1. Get involved with workers to find ways to increase productivity.
2. Convince others that productivity is a major goal of a firm.
3. Develop a long-term strategy for productivity.
4. Write productivity goals into budgets and plans.
5. Realize that gains come from doing things better and differently.

RESEARCH AND DEVELOPMENT. Another way to increase productivity is to commit funds to research and development. Research and development is crucial to the future of a nation's economic growth, as it is to the future of an industry and an individual business.

TRAINING. One way to cut costs and improve output is through training employees. Training increases an employee's usefulness to himself or herself and to employers. The skills, knowledge, and attitudes gained through training increase people's and businesses' abilities to compete more effectively and efficiently.

RETRAINING. Most companies have found that it is less expensive to keep people employed and retrain them for jobs that will be needed in the future. This practice has replaced the philosophy of terminating employees in low production times and then hiring new employees when demand increases.

BETTER MANAGEMENT OF TIME AND PAPERWORK. Better productivity can be achieved through reducing the amount of time spent in meetings by executives. Another area to focus on is the increasing cost of paperwork. Some possible cures include reducing the number of memos and forms, using electronic bulletin boards and mail and video conferences.

FLEXIBLE MANUFACTURING. The concept of flexible manufacturing can improve productivity. This concept means that a truly modern factory can produce several different products on the same assembly line on the same day. It is done by using computers and running assembly lines at high speeds for short periods of time. It provides flexibility, lack of large inventory, and the ability to meet the needs of individual customers.

ESSENTIAL TERM

Match the following essential term with the proper definition. The correct answer is located in the key at the end of the chapter.

A. productivity

____ 1. The GNP worth of consumer goods.

____ 2. The measurement of the amount of input needed to generate a given amount of output.

BRAIN TEASERS

Write the answers to the following "brain teasers."

1. Other than those items listed in this chapter, what do you think has contributed to America's decline in productivity?

2. Can you develop a model in which government, management, individuals, and unions might better work together so that the nation would again be a leader in productivity?

3. What has management failed to do to increase productivity? What can it do?

RAPID REVIEW

Complete the following sentences with the appropriate words. The correct answers are in the key at the end of the chapter.

1. ________________, ________________, ________________, and ______________ have been cited as factors that can lead to improved productivity for a company.
2. Organized labor has led to lower productivity through developing and maintaining a ____________ ____________ ____________.
3. ________________ ________________ is the basis for developing new plants, equipment and technology.
4. American workers have been ______________ ______________ in the last decade.
5. Individuals work harder when their work is ______________ and they are involved in ______________.

STUDENT EXERCISE

You will better understand how managers deal with productivity when this exercise is completed.

STEP 1. Contact the U.S. Department of Labor or Commerce. If you live in a large city, there should be a branch near you—look in the white pages of the telephone book under United States Government. If not, write:

COMMERCE DEPARTMENT
Commerce Building
14th Street between Constitution Avenue and E Street
Washington, D.C. 20230

OR

LABOR DEPARTMENT
3rd Street and Constitution Avenue, N.W.
Washington, D.C. 20210

Ask them for any information they may have regarding productivity and how business can improve its own productivity.

STEP 2. Visit a manufacturing plant or large service facility. Contact the person who is in charge of productivity (it will most likely be the plant manager). Interview the person and ascertain what actions they take to ensure that productivity is at a level the company desires. If productivity is not at an acceptable level, what steps or actions do they contemplate taking in order to raise it?

STEP 3. Compare your plant visit with government-recommended programs. Is there a difference? If so, why? Who has a bigger problem? Is the solution realistic? If not, why?

ANSWER KEY

ESSENTIAL TERMS

1. No answer 2. A

RAPID REVIEW

1. training, retraining, research and development
2. rigid job structure
3. capital formation
4. less productive
5. interesting, making decisions

CHAPTER

16 Management and Society

LEARNING OBJECTIVES

After reading and discussing this chapter, you should be able to:

1. Define this chapter's essential terms.
2. Discuss the meaning of responsibility as it applies to managers in this chapter.
3. List and describe the three phases in the evolution of managers' social responsibilities.
4. State two tests to determine if an intended action will be ethical or unethical.
5. List four ways in which a business and its managers can build into their organizations a true sense of social responsibility.

OVERVIEW

THE THREE CS OF BUSINESS ETHICS

What are the elements of business ethics? In actuality, business ethics is nothing less than the full awareness of what one is doing, its consequences, and complications. The three Cs of business ethics are compliance (living and behaving according to the law, corporate codes of ethics, company rules, principles of morality, and community expectations), contributions (giving customers value for patronage, giving employment, helping individuals and society to meet their needs, and making improvements to the quality of life for employees and community members alike), and consequence of business actions (either positive or negative for the company, society, and other individuals and groups).

TO WHOM ARE MANAGERS RESPONSIBLE?

Managers are faced with an eternal dilemma: They must balance conflicting demands as they attempt to allocate and manage their organization's use of scarce resources. The manager is in effect a juggler who must satisfy owner, employee, peer, competitor, vendor, and government demands. These domains are broken down into the domestic, economic, social, and political environments.

HOW MANAGEMENT IS LINKED TO RESPONSIBILITY

All individuals are linked to responsibility in one or more of three ways:

1. If we are asked to be accountable for our actions, that is a condition of responsibility.
2. Roles and rules we are required to follow are also sources of responsibility.
3. The concepts of trustworthiness and reliability also create responsibility.

Managers, because of their unique position in organizations, are the stewards of trustworthiness and reliability.

THE EVOLUTION OF THE MANAGER'S RESPONSIBILITIES

Manager's responsibilities have evolved over time through three phases:

1. The classical phase emphasized enlightened self-interest.
2. The social awareness phase, also known as the "activist" phase, saw government becoming involved and attempting to correct the abuses of the classical period.
3. The third and current phase is known as the social responsibility phase. This period stresses the moral and ethical content of managerial decisions. It is a very strong influence in today's business world.

MANAGERS, MORALS, AND ETHICS

The social responsibility phase of managerial responsibility emphasizes "moral and ethical" behavior. These two words are best defined as concepts of right and wrong that guide a manager's decision. They also set minimum standards for behavior. True professions have created a code of ethics that gives criteria for moral and ethical behavior.

THINKING ETHICALLY. Many of the decisions managers face each day have ethical considerations. There are eight guidelines an individual can use to think about the ethical implications of intended actions.

1. Consider other people's well-being, including the well-being of nonparticipants.

2. Think as a member of the business community and not as an isolated individual.
3. Obey, but do not depend solely on, the law.
4. Think of yourself—and your company—as part of society.
5. Obey moral rules.
6. Think objectively.
7. Ask the question, "What sort of person would do such a thing?"
8. Respect the customs of others, but not at the expense of your own ethics.

ETHICS PROGRAMS AND CODES. A large number of corporations have established ethics codes. To make a company program effective, the following is recommended:

- Greater commitment of top management
- A written code of ethics that clearly communicates management's expectations
- Programs to implement the company's guidelines
- Strict enforcement of the code
- Surveys to monitor compliance

MOTIVATIONS FOR MANAGERS' UNETHICAL CONDUCT. There are four basic rationalizations that lie beneath unethical behavior by managers. These are:

- A belief that the activity is within reasonable ethical and legal limits—that it is not really illegal or immoral
- A belief that the activity is in the individual's or the corporation's best interests—that the individual would somehow be expected to undertake the activity
- A belief that the activity is safe because it will never be found out or publicized—the classic crime-and-punishment issue of discovery
- A belief that because the activity helps the company, the company will condone it, and even protect the person who engages in it

Each of these rationalizations is just that, a rationalization. Each can be resolved by the company and management.

BUSINESS ETHICS TODAY: A REPORT CARD. Surveys have been used to collect the views of business executives on the condition of business ethics. According to these surveys, the top five ethical issues facing business are:

1. Employee conflicts of interest
2. Inappropriate gifts received by employees from outsiders
3. Sexual harassment of employees
4. Receipt of unauthorized payments
5. Affirmative action

In analyzing the results of other surveys, the conclusion is that even though there is a concern about ethics, America has the highest standard of business ethics. To improve on this ethical report card, recommendations have been made for companies to provide all employees with some ethics training and that ethics should be taught in every business course.

ETHICS TESTS. There is a difference between what is legal and what is ethical. A legal act may not be ethical. To judge whether an act is ethical or not, certain tests can be used.

MANAGERS AND THE LAW

Criminal activities in business include many kinds of illegal activities, from individuals who steal time and money from their employers to managers who defraud other businesses and the public through decisions to commit their companies to illegal paths or practices.

PROBLEMS FACING BUSINESS. The top five problems facing business are:

1. Theft of goods
2. Employee mistreatment
3. Procedure or policy violations
4. Vehicle safety violations
5. Theft of cash

Most of the crimes committed against a business are motivated by a desire for personal gain. Most crimes committed by business executives against outsiders are motivated by a desire to keep their jobs.

INDIVIDUALS AND ETHICS. Individual attitudes about ethics contribute to criminal activities. Polls have revealed that more than half of the people asked believe it is permissible to lie, at least sometimes. Also, the Internal Revenue Service reports that American taxpayers and businesses voluntarily paid only 83 percent of the income taxes they owed in a recent year.

CORPORATE RESPONSIBILITY FOR CRIMINAL ACTS. Corporations can be held liable, as individuals can be, for crimes involving intent. In recent years, this corporate liability has meant large fines and criminal convictions for corporate managers, board members, and owners.

MANAGING FOR SOCIAL RESPONSIBILITY

Many large organizations are now developing a variety of safeguards to promote moral and ethical responsibility. One of the efforts in this direction is the social audit.

THE SOCIAL AUDIT. The social audit is a report on the social performance of a business. Essentially, the audit is an effort to report on the social action programs a company undertakes. The report takes the form of a balance sheet/income statement that shows expenditures an organization makes toward meeting its social responsibilities. Activities can include charitable contributions, support of community groups, minority employment, pollution control, or health and saftey.

A LOOK AHEAD. As you complete this text and your course in management, you will have acquired some tools and techniques that will help you as you grow in the field. It is important to remember that the world of management is filled with great challenges and even greater responsibilities. Your personal integrity, your ability to function as a professional manager, and your "feel for things" will make you as successful as the efforts you put into keeping those skills up to a standard you can be proud of.

ESSENTIAL TERMS

Match the following essential terms with the proper definition. The correct answers are located in the key at the end of the chapter.

A. ethics
B. morals
C. social audit
D. social responsibility

____ 1. A report (feedback) on the social performance of a business. It may be formal or informal, quantitative or qualitative, public or private.

____ 2. Concepts of right and wrong that form a system of principles upon which decisions can be based.

____ 3. The moral and ethical content of managerial and corporate decisions is concerned with the values used in business decisions, over and above the pragmatic requirements imposed by legal principles and the market economy.

_____ 4. A branch of philosphy concerned with what is honest and honorable in human conduct, its motives, and its ends. It is based upon a system of moral principles and values.

BRAIN TEASERS

Write the answers to the following "brain teasers."

1. What is the difference between morality and ethics and law?

2. Why do you think that managers have moved through the three phases they have in terms of their social responsibilities when they could have begun at the third level?

3. What standard or test would you use to determine if an action is both ethical and moral in a business transaction? Is there a higher or lower test for personal acts?

RAPID REVIEW

Complete the following by marking each statement *true* or *false*. The correct answers are in the key at the end of the chapter.

_________ 1. Managers have always looked after their self-interest in making decisions.

_________ 2. A social audit is a way for a business to demonstrate that it is meeting obligations to community and others that do not show up in traditional financial documents.

_________ 3. One rationalization for managers' unethical conduct is a belief that the activity is within reasonable ethical and legal limits.

_________ 4. Ethics is concerned with what a good person would do in a situation.

_________ 5. Social responsibility, to be effective in an organization, must have the backing of managers at all levels.

STUDENT EXERCISE

This exercise will afford you an opportunity to watch and listen to several business persons and see how concerns for social responsibility and ethics blend into their professional discussions.

STEP 1. Locate your Chamber of Commerce and find when they have meetings involving many members of the business community. Arrange to attend as an observer. Do not inform them of your purpose but merely tell them that you are a college student and wish to observe how a Chamber meeting runs.

STEP 2. Follow any presentation and discussion listening to anything that might hint of concern and/or activities in the realm of social responsibility and ethics (you can also listen for other areas discussed in this chapter). If you hear something, is their concern deep or only casual?

STEP 3. Should you wish to pursue a topic you hear, question the members discussing the issue.

STEP 4. Write down your thoughts.

ANSWER KEY

ESSENTIAL TERMS

1. C
2. B
3. D
4. A

RAPID REVIEW

1. False
2. True
3. True
4. False
5. True

CHAPTER

17 International Management

LEARNING OBJECTIVES

After reading and discussing this chapter, you should be able to:

1. Define this chapter's essential terms.
2. Explain why business corporations establish foreign operations.
3. Discuss the influences of the environment and culture on the actions of an international manager.
4. Identify and discuss the variables an international manager must consider in performing the planning function.
5. Identify and discuss the three organizing phases through which a multinational organization evolves.
6. Describe the staffing and compensation problems encountered in international management.
7. Describe the influence of employee attitudes and communication on the directing function of an international manager.
8. Describe the characteristics of a control system and the specific problems of control in international management.

OVERVIEW

INTERNATIONAL MANAGEMENT

More than ever before in our nation's history, managers in all kinds of businesses are paying attention to what is going on across our borders and overseas. American businesses are part of a global economy, regardless of how large or small they are or where they are located.

THE U. S. BALANCE OF TRADE. In recent years, the United States has shown a deficit in trade with its trading partners. America's largest imports include automobiles, oil, clothing, electrical machinery, and agricultural commodities. Its leading exports are aircraft, agricultural commodities, data processing and office equipment, industrial machinery, electrical machinery, and chemicals.

FOREIGN INVESTMENTS IN AMERICA. Foreign investments in America are significant. Investment areas include manufacturing, retail trade, real estate, and treasury securities.

U. S. INVESTMENTS ABROAD. U. S. companies, in turn, have substantial investments in foreign countries. Much of the investment is in overseas business operations and real estate.

THE MULTINATIONAL CORPORATION. The growth of foreign trade means dollars, jobs, and tax revenue to the economies of states as well as countries. Nearly all of our country's top 1,000 corporations do business with, and have their own operations in, foreign countries. Many of these companies are classified as multinational corporations—companies with operating facilities, not just sales offices, in foreign countries. Thousands of our small businesses provide products and services to these large corporate customers. As the world grows and develops, so too will hundreds of local and national economies. The managers of those businesses that are part of international trade have become engaged in international management—managing resources across national boundaries and adapting management principles and functions to the demands of foreign competition and environments.

THE INTERNATIONAL MANAGER

To be successful in international management, managers must have certain personal characteristics. They must be extremely sensitive to the fact that they are guests of another country. This requires them to know and understand their host country because in most large countries that run operating facilities in foreign countries, a mixture of native citizens are hired along with foreign nationals from other nations. Thus, managers must have expertise in their host country's language, business customs, economy, and commercial law. They must also have a high degree of flexibility and they must be top-notch managers.

THE TWENTY-FIRST CENTURY EXECUTIVE. In scores of interviews with executives, management consultants, and business school professors, specific traits tomorrow's executives should possess were identified. These traits included:

- Global strategist: The future CEO must have an understanding of how to manage in an international economy.
- Master of technology: The future CEO must stay in touch with innovations and harness the new technology to make new and better products.
- Politician par excellence: The future CEO must deal with local and national regulation, international treaties, trade barriers, and changing currency values.

- Leader/motivator: Increasingly, CEOs must be able to assemble and work with teams of knowledge workers, pooling expertise and striving for a consensus.

THE ENVIRONMENT OF THE INTERNATIONAL MANAGER. In addition to business concerns, the manager must also be sensitive to economic, legal, cultural, and political concerns, not just of the host country, but of the total world environment. For instance, high interest rates in the United States brought concerns to European countries, but joy to Japan. Japanese products became cheaper and saturated American and European markets putting natives in those countries out of work. With the American economy robust in terms of high interest rates, European money flowed into the US, forcing European companies and governments to pay extremely high interest rates to acquire money with which to finance their companies and governments. Countries cannot operate in vacuums in today's world. International managers must be attuned to that fact and know what is important to monitor outside of their own companies.

THE CULTURAL DILEMMA OF THE INTERNATIONAL MANAGER. Culture is the distinct way of life of a group of people. To be successful, the international manager must know both his or her own culture and that of the host country. Only by knowing both can the manager avoid embarrassing acts. There are some fairly common characteristics of Americans and Europeans. They are

1. Individualism
2. Informality
3. Materialism
4. Change
5. Time orientation

The manager needs to find the common characteristics of the host country's people and must analyze five areas to come up with answers:

1. *Material culture.* Does the country have the technical know-how for producing goods? What benefits will they gain?
2. *Social institutions.* How do family, social class, business, and politics influence individuals?
3. *Man and the Universe.* How has religion and superstition affected the values and beliefs of the people?
4. *Aesthetics.* What role does art, music, and drama play in the country?
5. *Language.* Can the manager speak the language? What are its subtleties?

PLANNING AND THE INTERNATIONAL MANAGER

Planning techniques are universal, but the planning environment is not. To be successful in planning at the international level, the manager must constantly monitor

1. Political stability
2. Currency stability
3. Competition from state-owned enterprises
4. The desire for nationalism

STANDARDIZATION VS. CUSTOMIZATION. In the international market, a company is often required to develop new plans or adjust its present plans. As an example, American companies have produced standardized products developed for American consumers and then tried to sell these same designs to foreigners. But in today's global markets, customers around the world demand products with features different from those Americans find appealing.

ORGANIZING AND THE INTERNATIONAL MANAGER

Companies engaged in international trade typically create organizational relationships to meet their size, their state of maturity and immediate needs. Three stages of growth are common: the pre-international division phase, the international division phase, and the global structure phase.

THE PRE-INTERNATIONAL PHASE. When a company decides to branch out into international business, it does so because it thinks it can be competitive. Rather than creating an international division, it usually will select a group or an individual to begin planning for operations. They are typically assigned to Marketing.

THE INTERNATIONAL PHASE. When growth has reached the point that additional specialists are needed to run the operations and meet opportunities, an international division is usually appointed and the division is moved from Marketing to a position in which they report to a vice-president.

THE GLOBAL PHASE. Once the firm sees operations and sales on a global basis, the international trade function is assumed at the corporate level so that the impact of the international market can be judged on a corporate wide level. International organization structures are then erected.

THE BIG THREE'S FOREIGN PARTNERS. An example of a need to change organizational structures is exemplified by the joining of two or more foreign corporations. In the evolving business of automobile manufacturing, General Motors, Chrysler Corporation, and Ford Motor Company have all become involved in business ventures with international partners.

STAFFING AND THE INTERNATIONAL MANAGER

The staffing function of the international manager is almost identical to that of the domestic manager—trying to acquire the best people for the company. The international manager has two unique problems, though:

STAFFING PROBLEMS. Finding enough qualified personnel in the host country may be difficult, particularly in technical areas.

COMPENSATION PROBLEMS. An extremely difficult situation involves compensation. Since the company may have several nationalities working for it, should the company use an equity-based compensation system or one that looks at the needs of the individual? If someone has relocated to the host country should he/she get a differential over the native employee?

DIRECTING AND THE INTERNATIONAL MANAGER

Because people are so different around the world, the international manager may find that two distinct areas present problems.

EMPLOYEE ATTITUDES. Employees from different nations have different attitudes about the commitment they believe should be made between the company and themselves. Also, different nationalities have different systems for determining who should be promoted and how that process should be conducted.

COMMUNICATIONS PROBLEMS. Verbal and non-verbal language symbols vary dramatically around the world. Customs and common practices are dissimilar. A gesture, or a phrase, may have a positive meaning to one person, but be offensive to another.

CONTROLLING AND THE INTERNATIONAL MANAGER

The three characteristics of control, discussed in Chapter 12, are universal. However, unique problems exist for the international manager.

CHARACTERISTICS OF CONTROLS. Multinationals use direct and indirect controls. Direct controls include field visits by the home country's top management team, regular meetings to discuss foreign affiliates, and similar personal contacts. These can be expensive and time consuming. Indirect controls rely on written reports where return on investment and profit is the main issue.

CONTROL PROBLEMS. While controlling sounds simple, the issue of environment complicates the process. If there are several affiliate countries in the company, what criteria do you use as standards? Who collects it? How is it evaluated?

ESSENTIAL TERMS

Match the following essential terms with the proper definitions. The correct answers are located in the key at the end of the chapter.

A. multinational corporation
B. culture
C. international management

____ 1. The distinct way of life of a group of people; their design for living, which includes knowledge, beliefs, art, morals, and customs.
____ 2. Managing resources across national borders and adapting management principles and functions to the demands of foreign competition and environments.
____ 3. Companies with operating facilities—not just sales offices—in several foreign countries.

BRAIN TEASERS

Write the answers to the following "brain teasers."

1. Can you identify the three phases of multinational corporation development in terms of organizational structure? What are the major characteristics of each?

2. Discuss the problems surrounding compensation that international managers might face.

3. If a future international manager wants to get to know a country's culture, what areas would you advise him or her to explore in order to ask meaningful questions?

4. What is meant by "communications problems" in directing employees in international management? Discuss the concern fully.

RAPID REVIEW

Complete the following sentences with the appropriate word(s). The correct answers are located at the end of the chapter.

1. ______ ______ refers to the different perceptions employees have about a firm and their loyalty to it.
2. There are four basic elements which make up the international manager's environment; they are ______, ______, ______, and ______.
3. A ______ country is one that accepts a business operation in its borders even though the operation is not owned by a native of that country.
4. Political instability, currency instability, competition, and nationalism are all concerns for the international manager in carrying out the ______ function of managing.
5. In the control function an international manager relies on both ______ and ______ controls.

STUDENT EXERCISE

This exercise is designed to help you get to know your culture and compare it with another.

STEP 1. Pick any country in the world except for Canada or Great Britain. Using the materials in your text, develop a list of questions that you think would help you to get to know that culture better.

STEP 2. Collect answers to your questions. You can do this by direct contact if it is convenient or write a letter to a consulate near you. They will have materials to help answer your questions.

STEP 3. Fill out your questionnaire yourself. Let it reflect how you see the world in which you live.

STEP 4. Compare the two sets of responses. What areas do you see as potential problems for you? How would you deal with the issues? What areas do you see as similar or compatible? How could you use that area(s) as a "bridge builder"?

ANSWER KEY

ESSENTIAL TERMS

1. B 2. C 3. A

RAPID REVIEW

1. employee attitudes
2. legal, cultural, economic, and political
3. host
4. planning
5. direct, indirect